ROAD TO

The 12 Steps

MW00683251

PERSONAL STORIES BY PEOPLE WHO'VE BEEN THERE

EDITED BY DALE H.

FOREWORD BY DR. ROBERT J. ACKERMAN

PUBLISHED BY THE RENASCENT FOUNDATION

Copyright

The 12 Steps

Library and Archives Canada Cataloguing in Publication

The 12 Steps / edited by Dale H.

Issued in print and electronic formats.

ISBN 978-0-9947998-0-7 (paperback).--ISBN 978-0-9947998-1-4 (ebook)

1. Alcoholics--Rehabilitation. 2. Twelve-step programs.

I. H., Dale, 1957-, editor II. Title: Twelve steps.

HV5278.T83 2015   616.86'106   C2015-904945-8

C2015-904946-6

Cover by Jacques Pilon Design Communications

Print format by Chris G.

Published by Renascent Foundation Inc.

Dedication

This is book is dedicated to...

the thousands of men, women and children who've found recovery through Renascent. Your recovery stories let others know that recovery is possible and beautiful — even in the face of challenges that once may have seemed insurmountable.

our Guardian Angels and all of our donors, small and large — who support recovery by making charitable gifts to the Renascent Foundation. With donors by our side, cost is removed as a barrier for the majority who seek help but cannot afford to pay.

Acknowledgements

Editor: Dale H.

Publishing Facilitator: Roger C.

Editorial Committee: Anne P., Caroline L., Dale H., Jeff C., Petra M., Roger C.

Proofreader: Christine Sanger

Renascent Foundation Project Manager: Joanne Steel

Published by Renascent Foundation Inc.
Lillian and Don Wright Family Health Centre
38 Isabella Street, Toronto, ON M4Y 1N1
Charitable #11911 5434 RR0001

24/7 Recovery Helpline: 1-866-232-1212

www.renascent.ca

Table of Contents

Foreword

It is not often that we get to read real stories of hope, healing, love, resilience and recovery first-hand. The many authors in this book do just that and I am excited to introduce their stories to you. However, their stories are shared by millions and at the same time reflect the many journeys that many of us have made. Whether our lives have been touched directly or indirectly by addiction, dysfunction, or trauma, it is easy to recognize the physical, emotional, and spiritual pain that unmanageable lives can cause.

On the other hand, the joy of recovery physically, emotionally and spiritually is available as well to each of us if only we can find a way. Without a doubt, the Twelve Steps have provided guidance for our journeys and as you will read in this book, they have taken so many people from loss and despair to not only recovery, but a way to live life-long recovery, healing and joy.

I have often thought that one of the most painful types of lives to live is a joyless life. Obviously, people can survive many traumas, but without healing, each trauma can take away more and more "humanness," leaving a person an empty shell of a life. Each story in this book is a story of transformation. They are stories in which the author has faced a moment in his or her life that shouted, "I have tried everything to improve my life, but nothing has changed." Eventually, the authors realized that they had tried everything by themselves, believing that they could do it alone. No one recovers in a vacuum. We need each other and we need the wisdom of those who have gone before us.

Like so many others, I too believed that I could improve my life on my own. Fortunately, along the way, I realized that the quality of our lives is measured by the quality of our relationships with others and the ability to give and receive from each other. I am glad to say that at this point in my life, I realize everything has been given to me from others and from the Twelve Steps, beginning at a young age with Al-Anon. I honestly believe that my work today is giving away what I have received, and realizing that the hope, love, resiliency and recovery that has become part of me will not run out as I try to pass it along to others.

Finally, I would like to say that when it comes to recovery, we are our recovery. We either live it or we don't. Our recovery is based on beliefs that lead to healthy behaviours. Live it and pass it on.

Dr. Robert J. Ackerman

Bluffton, SC

USA

Introduction

My name is Dale and I am an alcoholic.

Twenty years ago, I said these words to a roomful of women in Walker House, Renascent's treatment centre for women at that time. I certainly didn't want to be there. But somewhere under the fog of my alcoholism, at my very bottom, I knew that I needed to be there. I had nowhere else to go.

Over the next 28 days, I would say those same words again and again. I would listen as the other women shared their pain, their fear, their anger, their shame and confusion. I would learn just what alcoholism was and why I could not drink "normally." Most importantly, I would learn that there was a solution, that there was hope, that recovery was indeed possible. Renascent has continued to be a touchstone in my personal journey of recovery throughout the years. I can never repay what they so freely and lovingly gave me.

Ten years ago, I was asked to guest edit a few issues of the Renascent alumni newsletter, TGIF Weekly Recovery News. Little did I know that today I'd be looking back on a decade of work as the newsletter's editor and have the joy of seeing the writers' contributions evolve into an anthology series of print and e-books.

TGIF was created in 2000 by Renascent Alumni Coordinator Lisa North as an innovative means of strengthening and supporting our far-flung alumni community by using the then rather cutting-edge technology of email and web browsers. In keeping with the 12-step tradition of storytelling, the newsletter (initially named tiktalk) largely consisted of Lisa's weekly reflections on recovery, supplemented by announcements of alumni events and sobriety anniversaries. The newsletter slowly evolved to contain interviews, relevant news stories and the occasional personal essay written by Renascent alumni, and was renamed TGIF.

Under the helm of Alumni Coordinator Charles McMulkin, TGIF evolved into an engaging, relevant and topical newsletter featuring lived experience essays written by Renascent alumni, coupled with contributions by professionals in the addiction and recovery field. During Joanne Steel's tenure, the voices of family members were strengthened and friends in the broader recovery community were invited to contribute their personal stories of recovery as well.

The juxtaposition of the didactic and the personal continues to be the foundation of TGIF. Videos, book reviews, poetry, special issues and Renascent outreach initiatives have all been added. But the heart of TGIF remains the personal stories told by alumni and others in recovery, from the newly sober to the long-timer.

Today, TGIF Weekly Recovery News reaches thousands of subscribers each week via email. All content also resides in our TGIF blog on the Renascent website (www.renascent.ca). Go have a look. There are over 1,000 articles and essays on just about any aspect of recovery you can imagine. Subscribe to TGIF while you're there!

As the editor of TGIF, I have long believed that these beautiful stories of recovery deserved a broader platform. Enter Joanne Steel, Renascent's Manager of Major Gifts and Communications. With Joanne's customary drive, passion and tenacity, these anthologies finally turned from dream into reality. Our volunteer editorial committee members spent hours poring through essays, looking to find the gems that best represent the limitless opportunities for growth offered to us as we live and learn in recovery.

The book you're holding features the experience, strength and hope of men and women who are living the reality of recovery each and every day. To them, we give our deepest thanks for their honesty and willingness to share their stories, their challenges and their victories as they walk the road of recovery with courage.

The "God question" has often presented a challenge to newcomers to 12-step recovery. Program literature makes it clear that the road to a spiritual awakening is a broad one, yet this essential truth can somehow get lost in translation. This volume reflects the experience of our writers: that spirituality can be experienced in any number of different ways.

You'll read stories of people of different religious faiths or none at all, atheists, agnostics, those who embrace other spiritual traditions, those who find their higher power in a higher purpose or through their creative spirit. All these voices and more are a chorus of hope and encouragement that you too can tap into "an unsuspected inner resource" on your own journey of recovery.

Essays written by Renascent alumni indicate the Renascent house they attended and the year they went through treatment. Contributions by our friends in the broader recovery community are identified by name alone. Renascent uses the 12-step treatment model (in conjunction with other treatment modalities) and, in accordance with the tradition of anonymity, all writers are identified by first name and last initial only.

The Twelve Steps of Alcoholics Anonymous

1. We admitted we were powerless over alcohol—that our lives had become unmanageable.

2. Came to believe that a Power greater than ourselves could restore us to sanity.

3. Made a decision to turn our will and our lives over to the care of God *as we understood Him*.

4. Made a searching and fearless moral inventory of ourselves.

5. Admitted to God, to ourselves, and to another human being the exact nature of our wrongs.

6. Were entirely ready to have God remove all these defects of character.

7. Humbly asked Him to remove our shortcomings.

8. Made a list of all persons we had harmed, and became willing to make amends to them all.

9. Made direct amends to such people wherever possible, except when to do so would injure them or others.

10. Continued to take personal inventory and when we were wrong promptly admitted it.

11. Sought through prayer and meditation to improve our conscious contact with God, *as we understood Him*, praying only for knowledge of His will for us and the power to carry that out.

12. Having had a spiritual awakening as the result of these Steps, we tried to carry this message to alcoholics, and to practice these principles in all our affairs.

The Therapeutic Effects of the Twelve Steps

Allen Berger, Ph.D.

The Twelve Steps of Alcoholics Anonymous have been heralded as the most important spiritual development of the past 100 years. It is my opinion that they should also be considered one of the most innovative psychological interventions of the past century. As evidence, consider the fact that the Twelve Steps have had more success in treating a wide variety of addiction problems than all other medical or psychological intervention or treatment programs combined.

What are the therapeutic forces that enable the Twelve Steps to help so many people who are struggling to reclaim their lives? My conclusion is that the Twelve Steps help us recover our lost true-self. They provide a framework that helps us work out a new understanding of ourselves and that teaches us a design for living that encourages authenticity and responsibility. This new design for living honors our basic nature. Working the Twelve Steps creates a powerful personal transformation that leads to a deep sense of well-being, serenity, and peace of mind.

A main source of much of our psychological distress stems from the belief that we need to be something we aren't — that is, attempting to live by the unreasonable demands of our false-self. We have alienated ourselves from our true-self in favor of an idealized version of who we should be. We've lost sight of the importance of character, people-centered values, keeping our integrity, authenticity and honesty, and honoring our true-self. We've made things more important than people.

This is the veer in the trajectory of our personal development that the Twelve Steps correct. The Steps help us wake up from the trance that our culture has created. They help us deconstruct our reliance on a false-self and guide us on an incredible journey of self-discovery and self-actualization. They help us clean house and make amends to those people we have hurt. They help us stay centered, grounded, and humble. They help us become authentic and present in our lives. They help us restructure our self-concept into something more positive, solid, and flexible. They help us recover our true-self.

Abraham Maslow made the following observations about the importance of a basic need like self-actualization:

- The absence of self-actualization breeds illness. (The absence of our true-self creates serious problems; it becomes a breeding ground for addictions and other forms of psychopathology.)

- The presence of our true-self prevents illness. (This is the most important protective factor against alcoholism and other drug addictions.)

- The restoration of the true-self cures illness. (This is the experience millions of us have had in recovery: our true-self is restored through working the Twelve Steps.)

The Organization of the Twelve Steps

The Twelve Steps are numbered for good reason. The optimal therapeutic benefit occurs when they are worked in order, because the Steps are interdependent. Each Step builds on the one that precedes it to create a powerful transformative experience. What happens in Step One creates an experience that readies a space in our psyche for what happens in Step Two. Step Two leads to what happens in Step Three, and so on. This is how change unfolds across all Twelve Steps. The Twelve Steps create a momentum that motivates us to honestly face ourselves and others like we have never done before.

Grouping the Steps

We can cluster or group the Twelve Steps into four functional groups. Steps One to Three form the first grouping. These Steps demolish the foundation of our self-destructive life, the one that didn't work, and build a stronger and more resilient foundation for a new life that works under any condition whatsoever.

Steps Four to Seven form the second grouping. These Steps help us develop a positive self-concept by encouraging authenticity and promoting self-awareness and personal accountability. They help us to become our best possible selves.

The third grouping, which consists of Steps Eight and Nine, helps us become trustworthy by righting the wrongs we have done to others. They teach us the nature of healthy relationships and to aim at having the best possible attitude toward human relations.

The last three Steps, Steps Ten to Twelve, form the final cluster. These Steps help us maintain our new way of life. They continue to promote self-awareness, self-realization, and emotional maturation through serving others and an ongoing program of personal and spiritual growth.

The process of working the Steps is like constructing a building from the ground up. You'd work in intervals and wouldn't move on until the previous job was completed. First, you'd demolish the old foundation because it was faulty, weak, and unable to support the new structure you hoped to build. Next, you'd dig a foundation and strengthen it with mortar and steel, and then you'd build the frame. In the meantime, you would constantly provide necessary maintenance to keep what you already built in good shape. In construction, it's essential to use the best talent and materials available. You wouldn't build something half-heartedly. And so it is with working the Steps. The Steps must be worked to the best of our abilities if we are to gain their full benefits.

The Steps facilitate a restructuring of the self. They help us find meaning in our lives and in our recovery by changing our emotional and spiritual values.

Reprinted by permission of the author. Allen Berger, Ph.D. is the author of 12 Stupid Things that Mess Up Recovery, 12 Smart Things to do When the Booze and Drugs are Gone *and* 12 Hidden Rewards of Making Amends.

Wrong Problem, Wrong Solution

JD M.

I am an alcoholic with strong addictive tendencies. Starting at age 13, I obsessively used drugs, food, sex, work, exercise and pretty much anything else that would help me to deal with my self-centred insecurities, shame and fears. Unfortunately, they all had undesirable side effects.

I tried many different medical, psychological and physical therapies for 22 years before I found the Twelve Steps. Some had given me temporary relief but none was a sustainable solution. My life got more and more painful as important relationships fell apart — you'd drink too if you had my problems!

However, since I started to practice the Twelve Steps, I have not only been abstinent from alcohol, drugs and tobacco but have learned how to use food, work, exercise and other behaviours in more balanced and productive ways. My relationships have improved. Therapeutic — you bet!

My 1950 edition of the *Concise Oxford Dictionary* defines "therapeutic" as:

1. *Curative; of the healing art.*
2. *Branch of medicine concerned with the treatment of disease and action of remedial agents in disease or health.*

Well, the key to effective healing is an accurate diagnosis. Properly understanding the problem often makes the remedy obvious. My Big Book mentor, Fred, summarizes the information in the first three Steps as follows:

1. I can't safely use (allergy of the body).

2. I can't safely *not* use (obsession of the mind and eventual relapse).

3. There is a solution and it is spiritual in nature.

4. Over-reliance on self blocks us from that solution.

I had been stuck in the first two of those propositions since the first time I got drunk at age 13. My friends told me that I should stay away from alcohol because it had changed me into an angry, nasty person. Yet I was drunk again the next weekend.

As the years passed, I had many experiences with self-imposed abstinence. No matter how great my resolve, I always eventually returned to drinking.

Before I got into 12-step recovery and met Fred, though, I didn't fully understand my problem. As long as I thought my problem was alcohol, I was unable to find a lasting solution. I could only try to treat the symptoms but not the underlying disease. What I didn't have yet was the information found in the Big Book, which describes the *spiritual essence* of the disease of alcoholism (Fred's third proposition).

During my periods of abstinence from alcohol, my reliance on other substances and practice of obsessive behaviours tended to increase. But, since my diagnosis was faulty, I didn't get the connection. I thought I had a whole bunch of problems and it seemed overwhelming.

When I was first exposed to the Twelve Steps and had my first inkling of the spiritual nature of our problem and our solution, I was terrified.

I have heard it said that it's actually dangerous to have the Steps displayed at open meetings, since any alcoholic/addict will interpret them for herself. Of course, I did that and what I thought they said was that I'm not only a drunk but powerless and insane and that the solution is to believe in God. I would be required to make a humiliating public confession of all my bad behaviour and then become a missionary.

My mind clamped shut like a steel trap. Although I went to lots of meetings, hung with other people in early recovery and even tried praying, secretly I felt that I was doomed. As the months dragged on, I became increasingly "restless, irritable and discontented."

By a stroke of good fortune, in my fifth month I met Fred, a long-timer, who explained the program to me in a way that not only made practical sense but also made me want recovery. The key was his explanation of the information in first three Steps — the diagnosis.

Fred assured me that I wouldn't have to make any public confessions, nor would I be required to become a missionary. He told me that what I *believed* was not important; it was what I *did* that mattered.

Crucially, he showed me the essay on Step Three in the Big Book (starting at page 60), which identifies the core of the problem as *over-reliance on self*, always trying to control outcomes and manipulating those around us.

Fred said that "spiritual" is about connection, particularly with other people. That's why I had used alcohol, drugs, etc. in the first place — they helped me to feel more connected. But I was allergic to those things. The Twelve Steps would guide me to a healthier, more sustainable solution.

Suddenly, everything fell into place. I had to stop playing God. I had to start to practice letting go of outcomes and begin dealing with others based on principles such as kindness and forgiveness.

With that, the real healing began. Fear and shame started to melt away. My spirit was waking up.

After years of practice, the Twelve Steps have become the basis for the way I live my life. They are part of me. They are what I believe in. Yes, they have been therapeutic in their own right but, more than that, they are the foundation for practicing these healing, spiritual principles in all my affairs.

Step 1

We admitted we were powerless over alcohol—that our lives had become unmanageable.

You Can Stop Fighting Now

Jennifer M.

I've always been a fighter. Throughout my life, I would stand up for my own rights or those of others. I would go after my goals with a fierceness only matched by the zeal with which I pursued my next drink. I saw myself as someone who could get knocked down in life, but would get back up again, stronger and better than before.

As years passed, and my alcoholism progressed, I clung to the idea that the answer to all my problems was willpower. After all, I had accomplished a number of goals in my life up to that point by determination and perseverance. Surely this drinking problem could be tackled in the same way.

When I first tried to get sober, I was 25. I had overdosed by accident after a regular night out at the bar. The next morning, still alive thankfully, I vowed that I would never drink again. And I didn't. Until two years later.

Thus began an ongoing cycle of controlled drinking, periodic out-of-control binges followed by more controlled drinking, a drunken scene that I would decide was the final straw, and yet another attempt at sobriety.

People who knew me suggested AA. I said I didn't need a program to help me quit drinking — I could quit drinking perfectly fine on my own, thank you very much. After all, look at how many times I've quit! When someone in my life finally suggested that quitting drinking wasn't exactly my problem, but that *staying* quit seemed to be a bit more of a challenge, I decided that I might need help after all.

When I arrived at my first AA meeting and heard Step One, I was confused. Powerless? Unmanageable? I was neither of those things. My life appeared convincingly managed. I could *manage* all sorts of things: my job, my home environment, my relationships. As AA's premise was an acknowledgement of powerlessness, the Twelve

Steps made no sense to me. I already felt as though I wasn't good enough in so many ways; now I had to admit complete defeat?

As time passed, and I attended more and more meetings, and heard other alcoholics share their stories, I began to hear my own story reflected in their words. The circumstances might have been different, but the negative thinking and self-hatred and sadness and fear? Those were the same, whether a 75-year-old man with 40 years in recovery or an 18-year-old newcomer was speaking. I started to believe that maybe, just maybe, I belonged here.

It took a couple of "controlled drinking" experiments just to be sure, but eventually I began to realize the truth of Step One: I really was powerless over alcohol. I had years and years and countless experiences to provide proof that when I marched onto the battlefield with my opponent alcohol, I was defeated every time.

That realization, that I was powerless over this thing, this disease, was demoralizing. I had been going at this all wrong! I had been taught my whole life that when you came up against a challenge or obstacle, you fought back. You fought until you won. However, when it came to the disease of alcoholism, I was fighting a losing battle.

And when I accepted that I was powerless, that nothing I could do on my own would rid me of this disease, I actually felt some relief. I could stop fighting. If I could accept that I have a spiritual malady and a physical inability to consume alcohol without experiencing the phenomenon of craving, perhaps I could start to move forward.

Still, acknowledging that my life was unmanageable took more time. I was certain it was only when I picked up a drink that things had the tendency to spiral out of control. Other than that, I believed I could manage just fine.

But as time passed in sobriety and I procrastinated on doing the Steps and stopped attending as many meetings, the unmanageability of my life became more and more obvious. I was no longer drinking, but I was still experiencing the chaos of my disease.

The drinking hadn't actually been the problem, as it turns out. The drinking was one of my many misguided attempts to manage the things in my life that were out of control: my emotions, my thoughts, my behaviours, my views of myself and the world.

Accepting our lack of power in our own lives and in the world at large is frightening. No one wants to feel helpless and ineffective, and I know in my case that my self-esteem had already been so battered and bruised by years of alcoholic living that I didn't think it could take yet another hit.

As it turns out, accepting my powerlessness and the unmanageability of my life is one of the many gifts that the program of Alcoholics Anonymous has given me. I no longer have to desperately keep trying to swim against the current, terrified that at any moment a wave is going to wash over my head and finally drown me.

Step One has given me the foundation I needed to rebuild a different life; a better one, as it turns out. Don't get me wrong: it's still hard, and there are days where my life still feels completely unmanageable. But Step One reminds me that it's okay, that I don't have to fight anymore, and that there is a solution. And that gives me hope.

Every Journey Begins with a Single Step

Jeff C. (Sullivan 2014)

If Step One begins with the admission of mental obsession, then I'm there.

I can see mental obsession in all aspects of my life, not just alcohol. That blueberry scone that was beside me, I had good intentions when I bought it. I asked for the china, no brown paper bag for me. I'm sober, I'm going to enjoy it like an adult, savour it like a normal person, nibble on it while I work. Now I'm hiding my plate on another table and thinking I should try a cranberry scone, just so I know which is my favourite for future reference. An hour ago I didn't even like scones. One nibble and suddenly they're an important part of my life. That's obsession.

Money, work, working out, relationships, sex and, yes, alcohol. I obsess. When I'm addicted to something, I can't stop thinking about it till I have it. I have suffered from a mental obsession with alcohol and other assorted substances for much of my adult life. This allergy has brought me to the brink of death on more than one occasion, the last being five months ago, in mid-July. A drinking binge left me depressed, shame-ridden and overwhelmed with anxiety. How was I going to come back from this one? And, did I want to come back?

I hadn't left my bedroom in five days. Five beautiful, hot, sunny summer days. Except of course to buy more. I wasn't answering my phone. My family was beside themselves. On July 17, an interventionist arrived at my door. That night, I was in the hospital hooked up to an IV. The next day, I was in detox. It was that quick yet that long; that simple yet that complicated. My family had delivered me to recovery but how I got there was all my doing.

I checked into the Sullivan Centre on July 21. I felt tremendous shame at that moment. It was a feeling that was no stranger to me. I'm well-acquainted with following-day shame. However, this would be different. There'd be no numbing the shame; I'd have to face it head-on. This is the moment my experience with Step One began.

Over the course of the next 21 days in treatment, I'd hear a lot about Step One. I'd learn that I had an allergy to alcohol. It was a disease. It was progressive. It was deadly. At first, this all sounded ridiculous. How could I be allergic to something that I consumed so readily with such pleasure?

But it soon began to make sense. By going over my own drinking history, I could see that, indeed, years before I realized it, I was out of control; my drinking was no mere habit and I did not consume like other people. I had no off switch. Like any disease, this one had its own pace, was taking me at its own rate and, left untreated, was going to kill me. I honestly came to believe that by the time I left treatment.

What is it like now? Since treatment, I'm like a tourist in my own city. I see different people and go to different places. I've even moved to a different neighbourhood.

But Step One is always there, asking more of me than any other Step likely will. From my perspective, that's a good thing, particularly now that I've completed my Continuing Care program. I feel like it's time to put on my big boy pants and live like a normal person, only not so normal. I heard someone once say that addicts are a little crazy. I can live with crazy; what I can't live with is the old me, the one that lied.

So, I'm closing in on five months of sobriety as I write this and I guess you could say I've drunk the Kool-Aid. I have admitted to myself that I'm powerless over alcohol and that my life is unmanageable if I'm left to my own devices. I've got a great sponsor and great friends in the program. I also have a program that's ever-evolving. I'm working the Steps on a daily basis, somewhere in between Two and Three and not rushing it. It's taken a long time to make a mess of this life of mine. If it takes a year to work the Steps and put it back on track, I can live with that.

Last night, I shared the following thought with a friend: for good or bad, addiction is a part of the fabric that is me. Given the choice today, I'm not so sure I'd change that. If I did, I'd be wishing away so much good that has recently come my way, including this very moment.

The Loving Arms of "We"

Máire O.

"We admitted we were powerless over alcohol — that our lives had become unmanageable."

My notion of "we" has evolved over the years in a way that reflects both the progression of the disease of alcoholism and my recovery from it and its effects.

As a child, the only "we" I was conscious of was my family. I was one of seven children in a larger family of grandparents, aunts, uncles and cousins. The kids were all born within a year or so of each other so "we" didn't want for others to make friends with. I realize now that with whatever was going on in my home, I was ill-equipped to make friends in school. I looked with perplexity at the girls in my classes who played together after school and on weekends. I really wanted to be part of all of that but had absolutely no idea how. So I came to look upon them with judgment and what I know now was anger.

Over time I started to "not fit in" — even in my family. I was a teenager, changing in ways that seemed normal but were actually outrageous. The unwritten "don't air dirty laundry" rule was so clear to all of us that no one spoke of my father's alcoholism and all its effects — the elephant in the living room. Fear, anger, hurts, disappointments, dishonesty, violence, doing without, were never really spoken about. I imploded. I sought solutions in bottles, drugs, relationships, geographic cures, all to no avail as my spiritual malaise deepened. It took 20 years to realize that these "solutions" were actually destroying me, as they had all my "friends."

There was never a really bonded "we" with anyone — until I walked into my first AA meeting, when something truly transformative happened. I did not consciously know it, but I intuitively knew I was no longer alone. Over a period of time, many discussion meetings and much fellowship, years of deluded thinking started to clear. I

27

saw that alcohol was the source of many of my problems and I finally admitted that I was an alcoholic. Admitting unmanageability evolved over time, with each new revelation of how little control I had over anything.

I worked the Steps as though my very life depended on it, for it did. I got, and remain, very active in service to the AA Fellowship, yet my life was still very unmanageable — not that I would let anyone know that. "Don't air dirty laundry" held fast until my breaking point.

I was just under 10 years sober and found myself out of control, trying to get out of a moving car on the 401, throwing dishes and pots and pans, overturning the couch — clearly not sane. Everything I cherished at the time, I lost. I had hit a bottom I didn't know was possible. I turned to Al-Anon with the fervour with which the drowning seize a life preserver. Once again, I intuitively knew I was not alone; I could open myself to the healing of the Twelve Steps of Al-Anon and that Fellowship.

Admitting unmanageability was immediate and continues to be a daily process. If it is outside myself, I didn't cause it, can't change it, nor can I control it. The parallel, of course, is that *whatever* I am experiencing, I likely have caused it, can control it and have the choice to change it.

The turnaround has been gentle, subtle, clear and profound. I am 100% responsible for my own happiness — and my own misery. Every moment of every day I have the choice to change my attitude to suit conditions. The choice I make is directly proportional to the amount of work I do on the Steps/Traditions/Concepts of both AA and Al-Anon, the number of meetings I attend, and the work I do with others.

"We" today is beyond anything I could have imagined. I am spending my Christmas holidays catching up with all my friends; people who have been in my life for years and those with whom I have just started to have a relationship. I need a couple of weeks to spend time with them all!

We do together what we cannot do alone. Ultimately, it is I who must make peace with myself and the God of my understanding, but I cannot do it without the loving arms of the fellowships of AA and Al-Anon.

Step 2

Came to believe that a Power greater than ourselves could restore us to sanity.

Hope Was What I Needed

Paul S. (Punanai 2011)

I lie in bed, staring at the imaginary blue worms on the walls. Three sleepless nights pass. The addicts beside me sleep endlessly. I am envious. On the fourth day a foreign feeling slides over me, an almost overwhelming sense that something is different. It's not regret, nor remorse nor guilt. It's defeat — utter and complete defeat. I close my eyes and pray.

Looking back now, I realize something about that stay in detox — that my best thinking, my absolute best intentions and my self-will had placed me in an abysmal state of body, mind and spirit. I was truly broken and battle-scarred. I could not do it anymore. But that important realization was offset with the dreaded thought, *How do I stop and* stay *stopped?*

For the first time in my life, I had no idea what to do. I didn't have an answer. Which is strange, because until then, alcohol had done for me what I couldn't do for myself. When I drank, I was Clint Eastwood, James Bond and Albert Einstein rolled up into one. I had the answers to questions no one was asking and I was King of the Hill. A sad, angry, lonely hill, but nonetheless it was *my* hill.

But soon King Alcohol would dethrone me and leave me a servant to the Master. I drank when I didn't want to drink. I drank when it rained. I drank when it was sunny. I drank because that is what I *did*.

At Renascent, I was told that there was a solution to my problem, and that plugging into a Higher Power would alleviate me of the obsession to drink. But I couldn't connect the dots between my out-of-control vodka-swilling career and this airy-fairy thing that would magically take me to a place where I didn't have to drink.

To understand and concede to my innermost self that I was an alcoholic was one thing, but to trust in something else other than me? And that I was insane? That was something else. But it was clear that I needed something, *anything* that would stop the pain, the self-flagellation, the suicide-by-installment-plan that I had going in what was once my only solution. I needed a new solution.

Being willing to believe in a Higher Power, a power greater than me, was key to a new way of life. I didn't even have to believe, just be *willing* to see that there was something outside of myself that I could tap into. And it didn't have to be the G-O-D that I had preconceived notions about from Catholic school. I could redefine those notions to what worked for me.

That is what turned things around for me. I could place the values of love, honesty, forgiveness, charity, and everything else that I wanted and needed and were in me but lost, into a Higher Power that I could rely on and plug into.

I realized that during all those years of clutching the bottle, I was asleep to a power that would fill the void in my soul. I was asleep to the one thing that would guide me to a life beyond my imagination. Knowing this left an indelible mark on me, as firm and profound as the marks left by hospital bands or handcuffs. *All I had to do was look inward and know that I was more than my thoughts and desires, more than my selfishness and worldly wants. There was something else.*

But what was this thing about insanity? I wasn't in a rubber room. I was an educated, well-travelled man! But my actions and thoughts were anything but sound or sane. Hiding booze, drinking and driving, hospital stays, getting arrested ... these aren't the hallmarks of a sane life. No matter what, I would still pick up and think, *this time it will be different*. Now *that* was the true insanity. I could not drink like a normal person. And that is what I had to understand to get this part of Step Two.

For me, Step Two boils down to one word — hope. Coming from a hopeless state, hope was what I needed. I needed to be willing to believe that a power greater than myself was the bridge between the problem and the solution. To come from a place where emptiness reigned to a place where a loving God would envelop me, would care for me, would guide and direct my thinking ... I never thought it possible when I prayed that day in that detox bed, waiting for the madness and the blue worms to disappear.

The Blue Angel

Kathy B. (Munro 2010)

Having no religious background, my heart sank when I read Step Two. I had come into treatment at 43 years of age feeling very determined and confident that this time, I was going to be successful and kick my addiction to alcohol.

I had been an alcoholic since my first drink at the age of 11. I had tried many times to stop on my own, and through various programs including AA, but had always failed. For one reason or another, I always drank again.

Before coming into treatment, I had a belief that there was something more than just us, but to call upon God or a Higher Power seemed impossible to me. I had done many terrible things in my life and had hurt many people — mainly family and friends, but mostly myself. What did I deserve from any God?

My understanding and acceptance of Step Two came from a very special counsellor at Renascent named Cathy. She and I shared an interest in angel collectibles, and one day I needed to ask for her help on a problem I was having with another resident. You can well-imagine that with 22 women in one house, issues and differences can come up. I had encountered someone who was just as outspoken and "always right" as myself.

I had always continued to talk to my deceased parents; they had always been there to pick me back up in life and I believed they were still doing it in my times of misery and distress. Two years before treatment, I was sitting at the lake having one of my little chats with my mom. Lonely, angry and very frustrated with my life, I was asking my deceased mother for help.

There was an elderly man fishing nearby and he approached my car. Of course, being me and not ever trusting anyone, I locked the doors and lowered the window only a bit. This man said to me, "I have something for you. You need it more than I do."

35

I sat stunned as this man went to the trunk of his car and returned with a small box. He handed it to me, smiled and wished me a good day. I sat there completely shocked for at least five minutes before I opened it. Inside, I found a blue stained glass angel. I was so shocked and surprised. Now I had proof that my mom was listening to me. After all, blue was her favourite colour.

I told this story to Cathy and she suggested that maybe it was my Higher Power trying to get my attention. Cathy told me that maybe I should get down on my knees and ask my Higher Power for help. Well, I didn't know how. I thought about that for two days, listened at meetings and classes, and finally decided to give it a try. What did I have to lose?

As strange as it felt to me, I prayed honestly and openly to God. Of course, I asked for proof, being the "bargaining alcoholic" I am, and never having trusted in anything but myself. I didn't have to wait long for an answer.

The very next morning, the person who had irritated me so much was calm and polite and just moved on to sit with other people. She no longer seemed so bad. I could see that the problem had been me being judgmental, and that I had totally missed the fact that we were all there for the same reason: to get sober and learn how to live again. I truly felt like the weight of the world had been lifted off my shoulders.

Step Two was the key to my sobriety. I came to accept and trust that I was never alone and that God had been with me always.

I thank God daily for all the miracles in my life. All I had to do was open my mind and heart, ask for help, and be honest. Life is not perfect, there are ups and downs, but I am five and a half years sober and for me, working the Steps is the way.

I had a wonderful sponsor for the first two years, Karen K., who continued to teach and encourage me about Step Two. Even though I knew and believed, she was able to remind me often of the promises being fulfilled by my Higher Power, who I choose to call God.

I will pray that if people struggling with "God issues" read my story, maybe they can just try it and see for themselves. This can and will open up a whole new way of coping with life and life's problems — if you just try it. The AA way has millions of sober alcoholics to prove that it works. Step Two saved my life.

Evolving Towards God

Max N. (Punanai 2013)

The first time I got drunk, I blacked out. If one were to gaze through a crystal ball that night, and the countless drunken evenings that followed it, it might show the beginnings of a crippling dependency. It was not how much I drank, or how often, but the absolute faith that I placed in alcohol as a solution.

I have always been a deeply spiritual person. Even in my most spiritually unfit moments, at the height of my active addiction, I drank fundamentally because I found in alcohol relief from pain, from life.

When I was asked to leave school, which was during my addiction, I had a GPA much closer to 0 than to 1. When I returned to education, a gift of sobriety, I learned of the idea of a hierarchy of needs. Though there are many theories that this may look like, it is widely agreed that the top of this pyramid is self-actualization — the spiritual enlightenment, in a sense.

Certainly, I drank to achieve the spiritual without the effort, regardless of the cost. The cost, in my case, was profound. My social life vanished, my ability to work and to attend school was destroyed, and my health took a turn for the worse.

Having made the necessary admission of powerlessness in Step One, it seemed only logically to follow that if I was powerless, then there was a power greater than myself.

Let's break Step Two down. "Came to believe" is a profoundly hopeful statement for any doubters, which most of us were at some point, as it suggests a gradual evolution towards God. While a white light might work for some, most of us experience the spiritual as a tide coming in — waves of understanding hitting us stronger and faster each time. These three words suggest belief is a destination we are seeking.

"That a Power greater than ourselves" is the second part of this second Step. As mentioned earlier, I had already placed faith in alcohol. Certainly alcohol was a power greater than myself. My reliance upon alcohol, however, had led to ruin in almost every aspect of my life. If I were going to surrender again, or change my higher power, it surely should treat me better than the disease of addiction did.

I remember sitting there and waiting for someone at the front of the room to tell me what AA's "Power greater than ourselves" was. When was the conversion going to happen? I needed to be on guard!

To my relief, these 12-steppers told me that I could conceive my own conception of my higher power. More shockingly, none of them really seemed to care what it was, as long as it wasn't drugs or alcohol.

"Could restore us to sanity" is the third and final piece of the Step Two puzzle. First, let's examine "could." It doesn't say "will" or "must" or "is going to do so by Friday next week" (however much I may have wished that). "Could" means that it is in your higher power's capabilities to restore you to sanity (more on that later) but he's not your employee. God helps those who help themselves, as the old saying goes. Doing the Steps certainly would aid this restoration.

What of a restoration to sanity? Well, could there be any doubt that I was insane? Sane drinkers do not have bars installed in their showers. Sane drinkers do not steal from people they love so they can continue drinking. Sane drinkers do not drink to blackout every night. Was there anything sane about my drinking at all? Hardly an inch, for the bulk of it was total madness.

Rome was not built in a day.

Step Two empowers, not enslaves, and it is with great joy that one, following admitting powerlessness, can begin to walk this incredible road.

Step 3

Made a decision to turn our will
and our lives over to the care of
God *as we understood Him.*

Meeting My Higher Power

Anne P. (Munro 2005)

It may sound crazy, but the beginning of my work with AA and my first steps on my road to recovery were inspired by the presence of a dog — a dog that wasn't even mine.

She was a beautiful and gentle yellow Lab; timid and wary of strangers but so happy around those she knew. She exuded the eagerness to love and be loved that only a dog can convey. Her name was Hawkeye, her owner being a M*A*S*H fan. Hawkeye had been abused as a pup and my friend, her new owner, was teaching her to trust and to let go of her fear. Hawkeye was on her own road of recovery.

If I regard Step One (my powerlessness) as inserting a key into a locked door and Step Two (coming to believe in a higher power) as unlocking and opening that door, then I consider Step Three (turning my will and my life over to the care of my higher power) as walking through that door. In order to do this, I have to have gathered enough faith, integrity and love to take me through that doorway — a daunting goal.

While I was in residence at Renascent, we were fortunate to be visited once a week by a minister who guided us through a series of three visual meditations. Each week he focused on one of the first three Steps.

Some of the images he talked us through as we sat with our eyes closed included a serene forest, a gentle rain and other elements of nature, along with images of our past and present selves. The first session was meant to bring us face to face with our alcoholism. The second session, a week later, focused on some awareness of our higher power.

I enjoyed these meditations and tried to engage my imagination as much as possible. I found them restful and interesting but not especially profound until, in the last visualization session, he directed us to sit on a bench in preparation to meet our higher power.

I immediately began to panic. I could not conceive of a higher power. Did I have one? I wasn't prepared to just invent "god" on the spot. Would I find myself turning my life over to some strange guy on a bench? How could I surrender my identity, my independence, my liberty, just like that?

In hindsight, my fears seem ludicrous, but I had been sober for only three weeks, the longest ever in my adult life. I was terrified that nothing could provide the reassurance and fulfillment of alcohol, even though my addiction had provided nothing but humiliation and despair for many months.

For some reason, because I was committed to either this particular exercise or my own recovery, I slowly turned my head to see who or what was beside me. This was my first act, not just of letting go and letting God, but of actually stepping through the door to my own future happiness and well-being.

There, seated on her haunches on the bench next to me, was Hawkeye. She turned to me and her eyes were filled with tranquility and ease, with acceptance and non-judgment, and with the kind of love that is given freely without expectation or fear of disappointment.

My higher power was speaking to me through this beautiful dog who was filled with simple wisdom, was learning to trust and was content to merely "be." I felt a relief like I had never known. I understood then that although my higher power was immense and boundless, here it was embodied, for now, in the form of an ordinary, genuine dog.

The freedom of surrendering my will and my life to unconditional love, to the present moment, to the guidance of something so mysterious and yet so familiar was the very opposite of what I ever imagined. The concept was overwhelming, but it didn't matter. All I needed at that moment was to allow Hawkeye to lead me through the door of Step Three and on to my journey of recovery.

Now, after nine years of sober life, I experience more and more of that relief and freedom. It comes and goes depending upon my willingness, my level of self-care and the strength of my faith, but it comes more than goes with every sober day I am fortunate enough to pass.

Then a Miracle Happened

Greg K. (Punanai 2010)

After acknowledging and accepting my powerlessness and unmanageability resulting from my addiction, I needed a power greater than myself to help me along the way.

Coming to believe in a higher power was a challenge in itself. By following the guidance of my sponsor, who has walked the path before me, I soon realized it had to be a power, any power, greater than me. That became easy for me considering the weakened state I was in, the powerlessness of my addiction and my unmanageable life.

Although I choose to call my higher power God today, it wasn't always so. In recovery, my first higher power was the Ontario Provincial Police. Once there were handcuffs on me, it wasn't hard to see they were a power greater than I was. I then moved on to my home group of Narcotics Anonymous with spiritual people who had 17 and 18 years clean and sober. They were surely a power greater than I was.

Then a miracle happened. A feeling of love, understanding, compassion, joy, empathy, forgiveness, purity, unselfishness, honesty, humility and contentment came upon me and I realized that just possibly my God was reaching out to talk to me.

Then came Step Three. Step Three states that we "made a decision to turn our will and our lives over to the care of God as we understood Him."

This seemed an impossible thing to do at first. Not only did I have to make a decision, I was to allow my will and my life to be taken out of my hands. I well remember my initial reaction to this concept and it was all fear-based. I was scared. I thought I would lose control entirely and be at the mercy of some entity I knew nothing about.

Most of all, I didn't trust. After acknowledging the problem and accepting that I needed help from a higher power, I now had to give up control. For me, control was the issue and willingly giving it up was something that I would not normally consider. Even though I had well-accepted my lack of control when it came to alcohol and drugs, I didn't like the idea that I had to give up having power over the rest of my life. Of course, today I recognize that I never had the ability to manage my life the way I thought I did. I never was in control. It was all an illusion.

How would I go about giving up my will and my life? Faith was the answer. This would enable me to proceed with Step Three. My sponsor told me that Fear came knocking at Faith's door and when Faith answered there was no one there. This meant a lot to me. It told me that Faith and Fear could not coexist.

But then came the question of how to put my faith and trust into something I couldn't see or touch. I was encouraged to understand that God isn't human, so I shouldn't worry about my typical distrustfulness with other humans. God is loving and pure and his guidance would lead me down the right path, if I would only let it.

It was then suggested that I think of myself as a pencil. I have the ability to draw beautiful pictures or write wonderful songs. All I need is something to pick me up and guide my movements. This is what God can and will do for me, as long as I ask for help through prayer and listen for the answers in meditation.

Many of us have said in prayer before . . .

God
Take my will and my life.
Guide me in my recovery.
Show me how to live.

I am an addict and my name is Greg K.

When I Stopped Fighting . . .

Ali A. (Munro 2007)

I always had faith — faith that I would be able to drink with impunity, faith that drinking would produce a certain effect, and even at the end, faith that something would work and get me out of the messes and wreckages I had caused in my life. I had to have faith, even if just a sliver. Alcoholics Anonymous was the last house on the block — the final option.

After realizing that this faith was within me, that there was still some hope, Step Three told me that I had to make a decision to turn over my life to a higher power. I had never really thought of anything beyond my selfish needs but I had something that was key — willingness. Without this desperation and an open mind to take the suggestions that the AA program offers, it would have been impossible for me to get sober. I had tried before, but old reservations held strong and true, and left no room for humility and the ability to let someone or something help me.

Once I had smashed the idea that I could run my own life, I had to find something that was going to guide me not only in my recovery but in my entire life. I wasn't sure what this power was going to be, but in hindsight it is clear that that power lay in the rooms of Alcoholics Anonymous. From my very first meeting, I felt something there. There were people who spoke my language and who had said that they had drank the way I had and now were sober — *contentedly sober* — and I could feel it. That power kept me coming back and even though I wasn't able to stop drinking right away, eventually I gave into it. I *was* able to put down the drink once I turned my life over to the rooms of AA and the people in them.

Step Three always seemed so elusive and vague and I spent a lot of time trying to intellectually understand it. What I didn't realize was that I was already practicing Step Three by taking my sponsor's suggestions, by running my "best" ideas by the women in my home group with long-term recovery, and most importantly by letting other

AA members love me through it all. The truth was that I really had no other options at that point. I had to give my life over to the care of AA first and then, through working the remaining Steps, to a higher power of my understanding.

I felt like a child again, having to rely on something else to run my life. That was okay for the first few months of my sobriety, but eventually I realized that by turning my will over to something bigger than myself I was, in turn, gaining independence over my life. I started to feel that I came into conflict less and less with people and essentially my entire attitude began to change. The acceptance and love that I began feeling allowed me to diminish resentment and made room for me to be filled with compassion and care.

But just how did this allow me to stay sober? When I stopped fighting with everyone and everything, I found that the obsession to drink slowly diminished. I began to hate less and love more. After five years of sobriety, turning my will over to my higher power is still something that I have to be conscious of on a daily basis. It's not always easy but I've found that keeping grounded by attending meetings and participating within the Fellowship is a big help.

I cannot afford to forget where I have come from and who I am — a recovering alcoholic. I still need guidance from something bigger than me, and even when life happens and I don't feel connected, as long as I keep acting out of the characteristics of my higher power (love, compassion, care, kindness, to name a few), I know that I am not alone.

I have to constantly be active in Alcoholics Anonymous and my recovery because for a girl like me, who will inevitably drink again by default, I don't know if the stars will align the way they once did — I don't know that if I go back out that there will be another opportunity to come back in.

I am grateful to have a connection to my higher power and to be able to help other still-suffering alcoholics; to pass along what I have. And when I align my will with my higher power's will, I live the contended sober life that I deserve and, most importantly, I am at peace.

Step 4

Made a searching and fearless moral inventory of ourselves.

Just You and Your Pen

Ben H. (Punanai 2008)

Throughout my entire life, I've always fallen short of being the guy that I wanted to be, thought I could be, felt I should be. I lived in a world ruled by compulsive behaviours and negative consequences. This started long before my first drink; in fact, it was the major tie that bound all of my childhood together. Drinking simply made all of it worse.

Just like all of my friends in the program, I did things when I drank that I swore I would never do. I hurt the people I loved, I hurt myself, I destroyed my life one action at a time, over and over again. I dug myself deeper and deeper into my alcoholic reality until I found the rooms of AA.

Before I found a sponsor who showed me the Steps and took me through the book that introduced me to God, I deeply hurt everyone I came into contact with who cared about me, over and over again. I destroyed a marriage to a woman who loved me very much; lost my home; lost my car and license; burned a promising career to the ground; and last but not least, lost all the feeling in my left leg from the knee down in one of my last alcoholic seizures. During all of that, I spent the better part of two years on the streets with nothing to my name except the shame I wore day in and day out.

I came into these rooms filled with nothing but anger and fear. I would lie in bed in the shelters and detoxes at night staring at the ceiling, unable to sleep without liquor and haunted by what I had done to my beautiful life. There was no peace of mind whatsoever without liquor because of everything I'd done drinking. So I drank to ease the pain but then I'd do things while drinking that would contribute to the list, making it longer every time I went out.

When I started working the Steps with my sponsor, it was proposed that we do them exactly like the book suggests and we did. I heard about the Fourth Step from so many people in the rooms; these epic tales that were pages long. Their dark secrets were boasted about like adventures, but I didn't feel that way. I felt dirty, used, sad, useless, dumb and foolish.

When my time came, I took all of that to the mattresses. I wrote it all down. All the fears, all the actions, all the darkness. All the things that made me different that I didn't want to tell anyone. All the foolishness, all the resentments, all the disgusting sex conduct, I wrote it all down and you know what? As I wrote it down, it all came out of me. It all stopped rolling around in my head, reminding me of the fool I was and the life I'd lived. It became de-charged and neutralized through that cathartic act of writing.

My sponsor gave me a deadline when I started and I kept it. I strongly suggest this to anyone new to sponsoring; it is what I do with my sponsees now. It gets you to the point and doesn't let you sit in it. Write down everything that comes to mind. No matter how big or how small, it will all find its place in your story. Go forward without fear because at this stage, it is only you and your pen.

Follow the guidelines as set out in the Big Book; they have served millions before you and I hate to break it to you sweetheart, but you ain't that different. I found this out as soon as I started listening to other people's Fifth Steps — the true meaning of "you are no longer alone."

This is never truer in my experience than when I'm listening to or giving a Fifth Step. The root of that Fifth is the Fourth, and you are able to do that Fourth because you have already turned it over in your Third to something that you came to believe in in your Second, which you were able to do because you admitted you were an alcoholic and your life had become unmanageable in your First. Funny, that.

So don't fear it; embrace it as a part of the puzzle that is designed to open us up to a beautiful world full of friends, family, God and other people's Fourths . . .

The Courage to Find the Real Me

Karen B. (Munro 2012)

I have learned so much about who I am and what makes me "tick" in the program of Alcoholics Anonymous. Being an alcoholic and an addict, I had lost sight of how to handle life and the challenges in it. I was acting on instinct. I seemed to have never gained the ability to take a step back and see how to handle problems with the maturity of an adult. Taking a good look at all the harm and heartache of my past was an enlightening and humbling experience for me. This is the rigorous honesty that Step Four demands.

Until I came into this incredible program, my life certainly wasn't about self-analysis — not of the positive variety, anyway. Nor was it about learning how to live in the best possible way. There was a lot of lying and covering up of my behaviour, just to get through the day. I lived in a constant state of self-pity and fear. I accused people and situations for all of my problems. I saw myself as a good person who kept having unfortunate things happen.

So I was asked to make a fearless and moral inventory of myself. What a task! I had no idea how to approach this. I was afraid of what I might see and how it would make me feel. I thank my higher power that I have a wonderful sponsor who put it into manageable parts that made sense.

I followed the example laid out in the Big Book of Alcoholics Anonymous. I made columns for my resentments, unhealthy sexual conduct, harms to others and fears. But where growth came for me was when I delved deeper — into the cause of the problem, my part in it, and how it affected my life — and I took a fearless look at exactly what I did wrong.

It took several months for me to get honest in this process. When I first tackled it, it was very difficult for me to look at my mistakes and own them. I felt sadness and shame as my truths rose to the surface. I realized that I was a much more resentful person than I had thought, and that my denial of the way I had been living was holding me back from the joy and peace that I was capable of feeling.

Believe it or not, in time and with coaching from my sponsor, I actually came to enjoy the process. That was a big surprise! She taught me to look at my hardships objectively. This is not a self-flogging request. It is bringing to light the truths that we already know about ourselves. I was now seeing the flawed behaviours that came up again and again and caused me such difficulty. But because those negative thoughts and actions were exposed to me, it gave me the opportunity to change.

During the process of working on Step Four, I was attending even more meetings than usual. I often went to a meeting before and after each time I would sit down to work on this Step. Listening to others share honestly at a meeting reminded me that I was not alone in my struggles. I had the wonderful warm blanket of AA and my higher power to protect me through my discovery.

As I got deeper into Step Four, I felt my burden lighten. I now relished seeing my part in my difficult situations. I felt released from anger. I learned how the same traits were manifesting in different ways, holding me back and keeping me in fear. As I worked through it, I realized that the people, places and things on my list were already being released from me. What a gift!!

Before starting this Step, I questioned how I was going to forgive and let go by writing these things down on paper. But as with every Step, when I approach it with honesty and willingness, I need to stop asking why. The answer is always revealed to me by my higher power, with the gift of serenity and peace that happens by working the Steps.

What does Step Four do for me on a daily basis? It is a tool that I can reflect on when life's challenges come up. They certainly come up, even in sobriety. But I can now tackle life's hurdles with courage and tolerance. And my higher power willing, I don't have to make the same choices that led me to fear and resentment in the past.

Step Four for Dummies

Larry F. (Punanai 2009)

The time had come. If I wanted to walk the walk, I would have to put pen to paper.

Many newcomers, I was told, had experienced the same difficulties. I had got past this "God" thing. I had gotten way past it. My years of drugging and drinking had taken their toll and there was little choice but to admit, accept and become willing.

But now there was that four-letter word dangling in front of me. My sponsor spewed the word from his mouth. I hadn't liked it said in the dark days, and I certainly hadn't grown fond of it in the rooms of AA:

Work!

But I knew. If I wanted to have the eyes of those who held medallions, not chips, if I wanted the steady hands and clarity of thought of those who had come before me, I would have to do the work.

Along my short journey, I had come to believe that those I came into contact with in the rooms were smart, even brilliant. And why wouldn't they be? They could divide 26 ounces into seven glasses so precisely that even a triple beam balance could not detect a difference. I was assured I was one of them. My story was no different.

So if I was so smart, why couldn't I get it?

The first time I read the Big Book (pages xxv to 164, this alcoholic's short version), I was 14 days sober. There must have been earth tremors during those days — the book shook violently in my hands.

As the fog began to lift and the words on the pages started to form sentences, I still could not get it, especially Chapter Five. I didn't like that chapter; it had that four-letter word in it. I also didn't get the illustration on page 65. I was frustrated. But Bill W. knew how to keep me interested. He splashed the word "sex" here and there. I read on . . .

I had graduated from university — from a prestigious business faculty. I knew what inventory was all about. I could account for stock, factor in depletion, adjust mark to market, post forward, and calculate the profit or loss. So why couldn't I get it?

My sponsor just smiled.

Jeff G. had come before me. I had asked him to sponsor me not knowing his path, just wanting what I saw in his eyes. My higher power had it all figured out. She had provided a Renascent alumnus, I would later find out, to guide me on my journey.

It was a sunny afternoon and Jeff G. arrived before I did. He stood outside the coffee shop awaiting my arrival. I was not late, but for work, I was not early. We entered the shop.

After the first cup of coffee, Jeff G. reached for a manila envelope.

Papers! Ugh! I imagined page 65, over and over ... words ... columns ... *work!*

From across the table and in front of Jeff G., I saw bold font on the papers. I noticed arrows, and even examples. Examples are good. I can do examples.

"Just follow the pages. It has it all. It's quite simple," Jeff G. said.

Simple. Simple is good. I can do simple.

"Don't beat yourself up doing it. Just do it!" Jeff G. instructed me as he passed the papers across the table. "It's 'Step Four for Dummies,'" he added, his teeth showing in a wide grin.

Jeff G. knew my condition. He had been there, done that. On his journey, he had come across those papers and kept them, ever awaiting the day of my arrival. All I had to do was fill in the blanks. I could do that!

It came to pass, and I ascended the Steps. Easy does it, keep it simple, first things first. I have now been there, done that, and am delighted to say that I have tasted the Twelve Promises.

As April buds, I am once again doing a Fourth Step. This time page 65 is clear and concise and, best of all, I yearn to do the work.

Those who have come before *know*. Those who will come after need to know *how*.

Step 5

Admitted to God, to ourselves, and to another human being the exact nature of our wrongs.

An Exercise in Trust

Paul S. (Punanai 2011)

"You're not a bad man, Paul," he said.

I tried not to cry as I turned away, watching the passing streetcars and teens playing on the football field. I was unsettled and yet settled. Finally. All I could do was try to take in what my sponsor had just said. I heard those words echo in my mind over and over again.

Not a bad man.

A bad man — that is how I defined myself throughout my life, throughout my drinking career. It was a belief that was as real and tangible as a plastic vodka mickey gripped in my trembling hands. The idea that I was a bad person was stained on my spirit like red wine on a tablecloth. The unshakable truth, as I saw it then, was that I was permanently broken. Defective. An unwanted item at a garage sale, destined for the rubbish bin. So why not drink to that? Or for that? Or *at* that?

When I shared my Step Four inventory on that cool fall afternoon, sitting on those high school bleachers, I wasn't sure what to expect. Was it validation that I was second-rate? Was it judgment? Was it about trying to manipulate yet another person in my life?

I knew deep down that it wouldn't be any of those things. My sponsor had shown me nothing but immense love and acceptance up until that point, so I felt safe in many ways already. On the other hand, I carried a lot of fears into our several Step Five meetings (I had a lot of inventory, let's just say!). Fears that had always haunted me and blocked me from the Creator.

Step Five was an exercise in trust. Complete and utter trust. Trust that I could share of myself — *all* of myself — without filter or façade. That I could discuss my darkest and deepest resentments, fears and harms, and not be rejected. For an alcoholic like me, all fears boil down to the big two — rejection and abandonment. And to feel either of those felt like death itself.

So to have my sponsor hear it all, and have him accept and love me further, unconditionally, was like having a dark curtain pulled away from my spirit. It was like a weight lifted off of me that would never need to return.

The greatest gift my sponsor gave me during this Step was the gift of empathy. Letting me know that I wasn't alone in my trespasses and feelings, listening with his ears and heart equally, sharing his own experiences when necessary, shining a torch of clarity on the fuzzy events ... these things taught me how to listen to others. How to take in their darkness and focus on the light within. Knowing when to talk and when not to talk. To hear the unspoken between the words. When to hold someone.

Step Five isn't confession, although there is a confessional aspect to it. It's about putting it all out there — to take that leap of faith and place our trust in someone else; in the Creator's hands. It's about seeking the truth — our truth — about what fuelled our alcoholism.

I saw how I acted towards others, how I harmed and resented them, how my fears propelled anger and isolation. I saw how my ego and instincts ran wild. I was able to see, with clearer eyes, and with my sponsor's help, exactly what the underlying causes and conditions were that pushed me towards the bottle.

I came to see that I wasn't that bad bogeyman I had made myself out to be. I wasn't a piece of crap that had me cursing at myself loudly and literally punching myself in the face because I felt I deserved it.

Sitting down beside another man and pouring this out to him put me in the vulnerable position of having someone know me fully and completely. Nothing held back. And to not have him leave in disgust was a great relief. And a first for me, as I tended to push others away because I feared they would eventually see the ugly me and leave me. But I was never ugly ... even if some of my actions were.

So, with his hand on my back, as I wiped those tears, my sponsor let me know that I, like him, was a good person. A man on the mend. A brother of the Fellowship. A child of the Creator. Another traveller on this journey.

Having that connection to another human being allowed me to grow in so many ways. I gained more humility. Acceptance. Grace. And I have used this experience to help those whose fifth Steps I've had the honour of hearing. When we share the exact nature of our wrongs and gain clarity through sharing with another, we start to move past the shame and anger that anchors us to our illness. It breaks the shackles.

Step Five showed me that I am worthy of love, that I am accepting of love and that I am the keeper of love. My old, unshakable truth was truly shaken, and a newer, gentler, kinder one put in its place.

We are not bad people.

Tearing Down the Wall

Heather L.

My ego would like to tell you that the first time I did Step Five I did it perfectly. I would love to say that I am a model AA member who put perfect trust in the program and shared all of my deepest, darkest secrets; that I went forward with perfect courage and integrity. However, that would be dishonest.

My first Step Five took place when I was two years sober. In the fall of 1988, I travelled from Niagara Falls with a carload of women to my favourite place in the whole world: Manresa Retreat Centre in Pickering, Ont. I had been working on my Fourth Step and was intending to do my Fifth with a priest. I was terrified.

The secrets I held on to were not only mine. Coming from a family of two alcoholic parents, shame and guilt were my constant companions. I learned to hide very early in life, which contributed to the isolation I felt. I knew that I was flawed and my family was flawed, and it was my job to make sure you never found that out. This was a burden I carried and drank to keep down for 14 years. I attempted to obliterate it and it almost obliterated me.

The *Twelve and Twelve* says that if we do Step Five we "shall get rid of that terrible sense of isolation we've always had." It goes on to state that "we still suffered many of the old pangs of anxious apartness. Until we had talked with complete candor of our conflicts, and had listened to someone else do the same, we still didn't belong ... Step Five was the answer. It was the beginning of true kinship with man and God."

If Step Five is to be done well, it needs to be done with integrity, congruency and honesty with both one's self and with others. However, if I was aware of integrity back then, it was a passing acquaintance. My life prior to sobriety had been one of survival, and there is very little room for honesty or morality when one is in survival mode. I was both unprepared and unwilling to share all my secrets, but I did make a start.

My appointment with the priest, that autumn evening so long ago, was counted off in minutes. I scribbled at Step Four, looked at the clock, fretted and scribbled some more. Finally, it was 15 minutes until my appointment time and I put on my coat and walked outside into the crisp autumn air. The coloured leaves dropped silently from the trees to the long stretches of grass. The autumn sky was turbulent with blues and greys, and geese flew honking overhead. I did not see or hear anything. I was completely locked inside my own head. I opened the door to the building and went inside. The door of the meeting room was closed. I sat on a wooden bench and waited. At the appointed time, the door opened and someone came out. It was my turn to go in.

The priest had on a black suit and white collar — that's all I remember. I pulled out my thick sheaf of papers: my Step Four. Many shameful secrets of my childhood came spilling out. I think I got to some of my adult drinking history, but was interrupted by the priest. He talked for a few minutes. He affirmed me with words I no longer remember, and then he placed his hand on my head and blessed me.

The walk back to the main building was surreal. Tree branches waved in the wind, spilling their beautiful leaves; the ground was cushioned yet solid under my feet; the sounds and colours and movements of the world around me integrated into a brilliant, incredible *one* — and I was a part of it. Suddenly, I understood that I was an integral part of the Universe, as was everyone and everything else. For the first time in my life, I was acutely aware that there was something, some Power that was wonderful and benevolent and that it loved me. Flawed, unlovable me!

That was my first step in dismantling the wall I'd built around myself. I have done several more Step Fives and I am about to do another one as I work through the Steps with a study group. The word "integrity" has become essential in how I conduct my life both internally, with myself, and externally with others. I no longer worry what you will think of me. My motivation in doing Step Five is to take out any secrets that are weighing me down so that I can expose them to the light of day. It is only in doing so that I can take down the final bricks of that wall I began building in childhood.

An interesting thing has happened in the meantime: as I take down the wall, I not only get closer to you and God, I also get closer to myself. My self-love has blossomed and I now have a place in the world with my fellow travellers. I am no longer alone.

Learning to Trust

Bryan B.

The first time I did a Fifth Step was about four and a half years ago with a previous sponsor. It was done the traditional way, with everything laid out on the table. The experience was a game changer — a turning point! The obsession to drink was lifted because for the first time. I was able to honestly believe and feel that something greater than myself did exist. And because of that, I was able to look outwardly and see how ego, anger and fear were running and ruining my life. That was a huge moment; one that I will never forget.

But like all moments, they come and go, and new ones are waiting to be discovered. And discover I did. From then until today, I have hit many highs and many bottoms. I have stayed sober, am still committed to my home group, go to meetings, meet my current sponsor every week, and I have made a few friends.

But during the past four years, I have hurt people. As honest as I want to be, I have lied. I have expressed anger, even outright rage. I continue to be scared. I have suffered through the deepest of depressions, so much so that suicide actually became an option. My self-hate was greater than any negative thoughts I had towards another person, place or thing. I hated my life, my existence. What had happened? After such a euphoric, positive experience from my Fifth Step, my reason for being was completely gone. And I was experiencing all this sober.

I kept going to meetings and seeing my sponsor. At meetings, I'd sit against a wall, lean my head back, barely listen. Just sit there and continuously remind myself of all the reasons I hated myself. It was gross, it was exhausting, it was frightening, and I really believed it.

My sponsor was and is my anchor; he stuck by me like nothing I have ever experienced. Because of him, I stuck to it too. He was the one person I did not want to let down, so I kept saying yes to his suggestions, to his guidance, to his kindness. I hope I never forget my sufferings.

Finally, through continued work, a little bit of clarity started to happen — months and months later, but I stuck to it. I started to get a little hop in my step. I was seeing a therapist and had started taking medication for my depression, but sobriety and time gave me the opportunity to keep trudging.

Through this entire experience, I came to realize that I have hurt a lot of people. That I am filled with fear. That I've engaged in unhealthy sex conduct. It kept gnawing and gnawing at me, "time to do a Fourth ... time to do a Fourth." But I kept stalling and stalling. The day did come, though, and I finally told my sponsor I wanted to do a Fourth and Fifth.

He was more than willing to help me out and recommended we do them in segments, meaning that in one session we'd do a Fifth on fears, and next time we'd do resentments, and finally sex conduct. Brilliant, I thought. Why bunch it all up into one? It also gives me time to reflect and think about in greater detail what was discussed and discovered.

First, he said, let's tackle fears. I went to work. My list wasn't long, but it was honest and it was close to the heart. Meaning big-time fears that really haunted me. I went through them, explained them all and also how they were affecting me. While I was talking, my sponsor was taking notes (he had a copy of my list), drawing arrows, circling words.

When I was finished, we paused. It was quiet for a few seconds. It was his turn to speak, and speak he did. He didn't say much because he didn't have to. All he said was, "These fears are from a lack of trust."

He was right; trust is my biggest obstacle. I assume the worst. I believe in the worst. I believe every outcome will be bad, so why even bother trying. He said, what if I trusted not the people, places or things, but my power that's greater than me? Trust that everything is going to be okay. Trust that I will get through it. *Wow,* that's what you call an "aha" moment!

He then proceeded to read pages 67 and 68 in the Big Book. "We trust infinite God rather than our finite selves." Brilliant. I may not like a certain outcome or response, I may not get what I want, but if I can learn to trust the spirit and not the "want," I just may improve on something here.

Simplicity can be seen only when someone shows me. It's a simple process, trusting my higher power. Now it's time to put it into action. And that's a whole other ball game, but at least I have something in my back pocket now. At least I have a little more wisdom to take with me. And if or when a moment of fear comes upon me, I hope I can remember to trust my spirit that everything is going to be okay, and that I will get through it.

Step 6

Were entirely ready to have God remove all these defects of character.

Taking the Garbage Out

Tony A.

God drives the garbage truck ... and I pray for the willingness to take the garbage out.

My first attempt at working Step Six was a bit convoluted, I must say. I was so delighted with the feelings of release and elation from just having done Step Five with my sponsor, and was so dreading my coming work with Steps Eight and Nine, that I think I really did not understand the impact of Steps Six and Seven at the time. I also don't think that I fully trusted God or the power of the Steps in the manner that was necessary to embrace the work of change, but I made a beginning and that was important.

Having learned very clearly of my character defects from a rigorous and thorough examination with my sponsor in my Step Five work, I was then asked to reflect upon them and become "entirely ready" to have all of them removed. In theory, this seems like a walk in the park. However, this hasn't been the case with me.

Many of these defects I have lived with for much of my life, both the objectionable ones that cause me grief and the ones that give me benefit or pleasure. As I've journeyed along in sobriety, the more sublime character defects that "seemed" to not be so glaring at the time have reared their ugliness as I've continued uncovering and discovering what is actually blocking me. I work and rework these Steps, and each time the truth becomes more visible and real for me, and more is revealed.

The process is so exciting and fundamentally good for an alcoholic of my type. What I at first thought was a process of becoming perfect and "getting good" has really been a process of letting go and surrendering, particularly in terms of *perfection* and *ego.*

I have heard it said our defects are like survival skills that are no longer serving us. Many of these defects will cause me pain and suffering in my sober life, in particular with my personal relations.

This is very true for me, as many of my defects are an offshoot of the "parent" defects of selfishness and self-centredness. When the pain of living in these defects becomes more unbearable and embarrassing than the fear of letting them go, I am then in a ripened position to be entirely ready to have my higher power remove them.

My work in Step Six depends on how earnestly I have made the decision to turn my will and my life over to the care of God as I understand God in Step Three. Step Six reminds me that I am powerless to remove these defects on my own and that I am in a partnership with a power greater than myself. I really need to make the commitment to have God remove these defects — this is the deal in Step Six. I am to accept myself as I am, flaws and all, and become willing to let go of all that stands in the way of my health, growth and usefulness. No other action is needed, as the rest is up to my higher power.

"Let go and let God" is the essence of Step Six for me, and I use this mantra in my meditation practice as a reinforcement to continue with my willingness to be entirely ready. When I fall short of my values and ideals in my spiritual journey, I continue to pray for this willingness. Today, there certainly is more depth and weight to this practice, cultivating much deeper layers of honesty and willingness.

I am also reminded that my higher power removes these defects, not me, and my part is to try to remain open and willing and to stay on course. All that I can do is pack up the garbage and bring it to the curb to keep my house from getting smelly. I then need to exercise patience, since God is in charge and he really does do the work in the next Step.

The inner blessing of Step Six through its spiritual principle of "willingness" is that of deepening my faith and trust in a higher power. I need not struggle alone, attempting the impossible. I am reminded that God can and will do for me what I cannot do for myself — when I let him.

Ready or Not, Here I Come!

Leslie H. (Munro 2003)

You know that line from the childhood game of hide-and-seek? The one where, if we were *it*, and we had madly counted to 100, and every fibre of our being was on high alert, we'd scream out, "READY OR NOT, HERE I COME!"? I know you know it.

Well, it's got nothing and everything to do with Step Six. It's like the line in the text (page 53) that tells us "that either God is everything or else He is nothing. God either is, or He isn't." So, it's like this with Step Six ... we're either ready (to take this Step) or we're not.

How do I know if I'm ready, though?

I am ready if I've carried out the first five proposals to the best and fullest of my ability. I'm ready if I've left nothing out. I return home from my Fifth Step, take that quiet hour, take the book down from the shelf, have a "look" at Step Six in light of this moment, and when ready, take Step Seven by saying the prayer. For me, it's that simple.

Content with patient improvement

The *Twelve Steps and Twelve Traditions* tells me that "Step Six — 'Were entirely ready to have God remove all these defects of character' — is A.A.'s way of stating the best possible attitude one can take in order to make a beginning on this lifetime job" and that I need to be "content with patient improvement" as I respond to my Higher Power's invitation to "try as best [as I] know how to make progress in the building of character."

It's not always readily apparent when or how my Higher Power will choose to help me work on the removal of my defects of character. I do believe that Step Six is like gardening ... I need to be ready and I need to know that it takes time to cultivate and grow ... and that it takes regular, persistent work and lots of love and firm gentleness.

Over ... and over ... and over again

In the first years of my recovery, I just kept working away at Steps Four and Five; my Steps Six and Seven were more or less glossed over. It wasn't until I started working with my current sponsor five years ago that I learned precisely how to work Steps Six and Seven straight out of the book, boom, done. One paragraph on Six and one paragraph on Seven with its prayer and done. Immediately I moved into Steps Eight and Nine. Over and over again.

It's only been in retrospect, with my repeated Fours, that I can see patterns emerging with my chief defect(s). I have come to understand that there are only a handful of defects to choose from. Where had I been: 1) selfish; 2) dishonest; 3) self-seeking and frightened; and 4) (the fallback) inconsiderate? That's it. Under those headings, all sorts of other minor defects fall. It was big for me to come to know this.

Expect (and give thanks in advance for) the opposite

Personally, I don't think our defects are removed. I think they're assimilated and I think this outlook speaks to how our liabilities are turned into assets. I have to do my part in this process: the Steps, my prayer, my meditation, my continued check-ins with my sponsor, my meetings, my working with others, my growing desire to put others ahead of me.

Two of my main character defects are being self-seeking and being frightened. Through persistent work, I have come to understand what I'm working toward in their "removal" or healing. I am working toward the opposite: being God-seeking and loving.

These particular defects — originally survival skills — have been with me for most of my life, since I was a little one. Today, I am ready to look at that wounded little one, to have compassion for her, and to seek my Higher Power's help in caring for both of us (Step Three). Today, there is evidence of "patient improvement" in this — a willingness to pause in times of uncertainty or emotional disturbance, to take actions to help me reground, re-centre, and reconnect with my HP. I am mindful that I don't get better overnight.

Today, I get to see that others may be just like me — self-seeking and frightened — and I get to be part of the solution in tandem with them, because today, increasingly, I recognize my own traits in others, and today, having the beginnings of compassion for myself, I get to extend that to others.

Increasingly, as a workmate often lovingly teases me, I am assimilating into someone who loves being in her own skin! Sober and ready for anything — what a trip and what a miracle! Are *you* ready?

Peeling the Onion

Drew M. (Sullivan 2007)

I've learned that Step Six has several parts to it for me.

First, I must write about the things I have done and the ways I have acted that bother me or that I don't like about myself. I then need to write the reasons for what I did, and why I think I did them. I need to understand what I was feeling and why I was feeling that way. Then I can identify those feelings as character defects.

Second, once I'm aware of the behaviours and character defects that I don't like about myself, I can see when and how I act out on those defects and behaviours. Being aware of this will help me to make the changes I want to make in my life. If I don't know when or why I do the things that I do, how can I change them?

Finally, I need to ask the God of my understanding for help to take the action necessary to change those character defects and bad behaviours. I know that God will give me the tools to change the things I need to change in my life, but it is up to me to use those tools and take the action to change. The God of my understanding will not do it for me. I know that when I'm living a spiritual life and following the will of the God of my understanding, I am allowing him to help me remove my character defects.

I've done Steps Six and Seven a few times now, and find it amazing how things change for me each time I do them.

On my first kick at the can, I looked at my angers and fears and the pain I had in my life. I was resentful and took no responsibility for my own actions in my life. I looked deep inside myself to understand why I did the things I did. With the support of my sponsor and some great friends and family, I was helped to see some of my character defects. When I could see my defects, I was able to let go and move forward from the old behaviours that were still affecting me. I was able to let go and trust the God of my understanding and face my criminal past in court.

The next time I did my Sixth and Seventh Steps, I had been clean for about a year and had to learn to deal with people, society and people in the fellowship. Character defects can come back, and new ones are always developing. I found that ego, pride and being judgmental were beginning to creep back into my life. The Sixth Step helped me to turn those defects into spiritual principles. I let the God of my understanding give me courage, understanding and compassion for others. I found that having humility for myself and others kept me humble and focused on a spiritual path.

I've found that each time I go back and do my Steps, I can go a bit deeper into my past and find more things I want to change about myself. It is true what they say, that an addict's life is like an onion. When you tear away one layer of the onion, there are more underneath to be discovered. I've found for myself that when I know what my character defects are, then I can start to change them.

I believe the goal of the Sixth Step is simply to figure out who I am and to change what I don't like. This step is the beginning of turning around my life and turning my will and actions toward a more spiritually centred path.

Step 7

Humbly asked Him to remove our shortcomings.

Little by Slowly

Paul S. (Punanai 2011)

Yesterday, we had a storm that cut the power at my place of work. As I left to make my way home, the elevator opened and out came a staff member who had been trapped in the elevator for several hours in between floors. She was teary-eyed. I immediately grabbed her some water and tissues and asked if she needed anything else. She said she just wanted to go home and was afraid to get back on that same elevator. I offered to go with her, as I was leaving too. And down we went — safely.

I write about this because in my active days, I would never have offered any assistance. I would have walked past her, knowing she was in distress, but busy with my own self-centred worries and random musings. My thoughts often trapped me and my spirit often descended downwards, just like that elevator.

In this mindset, my needs came first, and the thought of helping others was as foreign to me as writing a novel in Sanskrit or playing the lute. The only time I would offer myself was when the outcome favoured me, or when it briefly bolstered my self-esteem or ego.

This new-found spiritual sleight of hand didn't come overnight, though. Although I identified my character defects in Steps Four and Five, it wasn't until I got to Steps Six and Seven that I was able to let the Creator tackle those defects. Step Six asks me if I am entirely ready to have these things removed. And in Step Seven, I *humbly* ask him to remove my shortcomings.

So humility is involved — something new to me. I ask Him to take things like my selfishness, my fear of failure, my playing the victim card, my sarcasm, my grandiosity, my low self-esteem, etc.

Then what? I can't sit down and expect all those things to magically vanish like Copperfield tackling a field of bunnies. I can't work on myself — I tried that while drinking and that went pear-shaped quickly. I had bookshelves lined with self-help books. They did nothing but keep me in the delusion that I could save myself; that ego was running the show. And the Steps are everything but self-help — this is Higher Power-propelled stuff. I am out of the equation. So then what do I *do* in this Step?

For this alcoholic, the answer is a simple yet profound one. I keep myself open to His guidance. And how do I do that? I keep the noise away. I stay teachable and willing to do what I need to do to stay well. I do the Step work, help others and keep myself on an even spiritual plane. I listen to that little voice — you know, the one that tells you what is the right thing to do. Call it intuition, conscious contact, whatever. When I listen and move past the fear of not doing it, and *do* it, I am allowing my Higher Power to remove my shortcomings, as He sees them.

In conjunction with that, I often *act* as if the character defect has been removed. He removes the things that block me from Him through action. If I see someone who needs help getting on the bus, or if I can give a ride to someone in poor weather, or even sit down with a friend in need, I do it. I don't overthink it. I don't let ego hold sway. Before I know it, selfishness starts to dissipate. Through action, through His gentle nudging.

This is the beautiful thing about Step Seven — it's not about force and will. It's not about cramming a round peg into a square hole. This is about riding along the gentle current that is borne within us and through us that brings us to place of serenity and peace. It's about swaying and staying with our inner calling navigated by Him, to a destination we are not privy to at the moment, but we know is meant for us and us alone. It's about having the faith and courage to move against our own ego-driven tide and place trust in the process. My character defects dissolve little by slowly. It's over a lifetime that I get to reap the benefits of this Step, contingent on my willingness.

And like that young lady in the elevator, I get to continue my journey home, feeling safe and sound, rehydrated by the Sunlight of the Spirit and knowing that every move forward is a move away from the drink, and closer to Him.

Knowing Who I Am

Debbie F.

When I did my first Fourth Step and then my Fifth Step with my sponsor, I discovered that I had character defects. While I always knew there was something wrong with me, I believed I was permanently damaged by my past and my only hope was intense therapy with a professional. Steps Four and Five led me to the following steps and a new hope that I could change.

The first time I approached the Seventh Step, I was eager and very willing to complete it. I believed then that all my defects would be miraculously taken away from me, never to return, just because I asked. Then I would really become the saint I always wanted to be — and sometimes thought I was.

However, as I continued to enjoy my new-found sobriety and grow in the program, I realized that many, if not all, of my character defects were still present in varying degrees.

When I was drinking, my life experiences were very limited. But with increasing sobriety, I was able to challenge myself and explore changes that I could never consider before. While this was exciting, I noticed certain defects rearing their ugly heads as I ventured out in the world.

I needed to take a step back, take an inventory of how I was feeling about the situation and identify the character defect it brought up. Sometimes I was able to do this alone; sometimes I needed to discuss it with another AA person. Either way, I came to accept that this was the best way for me to deal with my defects — one at a time — when they caused me difficulty or pain. Pain has always been and continues to be a great motivator for me to act.

The first word in this step is "Humbly," and Step Seven is all about humility. I had difficulty with this word. As a child, I experienced many humiliating experiences that left me with a lot of shame.

Exploring this word in the dictionary, I came to understand humility as simply knowing who I am, good and bad. While some of my past experiences did in fact shape the person I became, I began to realize that my character defects kept me stuck there.

Pride is a major defect of mine. I lived my life taking credit for my good qualities and ignoring the bad ones by blaming someone else for my problems. I used the wrongs done to me to justify all kinds of bad behaviour, leading me to hate myself more and more. I believe this is what eventually led me to my alcoholism.

This has not been easy for me and I continue to struggle with some of my shortcomings. When I came to AA just over 20 years ago, I knew I wanted and needed a new life if I was to gain and maintain sobriety. Getting sober was not easy for me and the compulsion to drink took a long time to leave.

Although I was very angry when I first came around, desperation made me humble. That humility made it possible to rely on a higher power and AA to get sober. As I got better, I stayed sober and enjoyed a new life.

As long as things are going along smoothly, it's not too difficult. But life doesn't always go smoothly and this often brings up a defect I need to work on. The *Twelve and Twelve* states, "The chief activator of our defects has been self-centered fear — primarily fear that we would lose something we already possessed or would fail to get something we demanded" (page 76). When I am disturbed about something, what is it that I am not accepting and why? I can do an inventory of myself, identify the defect and humbly ask my higher power to remove it.

Today, I am sober. I have learned to live without alcohol. But I still struggle with a living problem. Life brings new challenges daily and if I am going to have contented sobriety, I need to learn to live with the things I cannot change.

One of the ways I do this is by changing myself. With a new-found humility, a higher power and the AA program, I can do this "one day at a time."

Learning to Hit the Reset Button

JD M.

Step Seven: "Humbly asked Him to remove our shortcomings."

Easy Step, I thought. Recite a simple prayer. Ten seconds at most. Then, as the Big Book says, "We have then completed Step Seven" and we move on to make amends.

Boy, have my understanding and especially my practice of this Step sure changed over the years. It has become the Step that, next to Step One, is most central to my maintenance of a fit spiritual condition.

The keys are all there in the Seventh Step prayer:

"My Creator, I am now willing that you should have all of me, good and bad. I pray that you now remove from me every single defect of character which stands in the way of my usefulness to you and my fellows. Grant me the strength, as I go out from here, to do your bidding."

Perhaps the most profound change in my program from its early days has been my understanding of the term "defects of character." When I first started to look at AA's Twelve Steps, I already thought of myself as hugely defective. That term seemed like an invitation to further shame myself; to pick away at old scabs.

And I felt hopeless when I heard people sharing at meetings, saying that they had defects like fear, over-sensitivity, willfulness and selfishness — and even an ongoing desire to drink. Am I really going to be fearless and selfless? We think not!

Over time, though, I picked up clues from various sources that have led me to a more practical understanding of character defects. I now see them primarily as defense mechanisms that I use to cope with situations that feel unsafe. Developed in childhood, they make use of my best innate skills and aptitudes to try to manipulate the people around me and the situations I encounter or perceive. And I've honed those behaviours through decades of practice.

In this context, fear (or sadness or loneliness) is *not* a defect of character — it is a natural feeling that is there for a reason. It is my *response* to fear that can be "defective."

My over-sensitivity isn't a defect; it's just part of who I am. But it tends to exaggerate my feeling of fear (or sadness or loneliness), so that my defenses are too easily triggered. And since my defenses are based on a childlike self-centredness in an attempt to manipulate the world around me, they tend to drive other people away, to destroy my connections to the world. The world responds accordingly and I feel even more fearful, lonely and sad.

In this context, that middle sentence of the Seventh Step prayer makes much more sense. What I'm asking for is to change my behaviour so that I can be of service, connected to the world and its people. It is a natural development from Steps Four and Five, where I get to look at and start to understand my conduct (especially when triggered by resentments and fears), and from Step Six, where I become willing to explore new, more mature behaviours.

Step Six has involved a ton of work for me outside of AA, including involvement in programs like ACoA, CoDA and Al-Anon, as well as various forms of therapy. Each of these has given me new awareness, new language and new practice. This Step has helped me to see the true me, how and why I behave as I do, and has started to give me some grace — which I experience as an awareness or feeling; a moment where I have a chance to stop or to do it differently.

Grace is a gift that I can work hard for, but my hard work is not enough. Once again, I can try to manipulate the outcome. I can get discouraged and resentful when I don't get quick results or, worse, when I have previously had good results but then take a step backward. I can beat myself up big-time, which just makes it worse. This is where Step Seven comes into play, as outlined in the first and third sentences of the Seventh Step prayer.

I practiced those old self-centred ways for decades. If I'm hungry, angry, lonely or tired (especially tired) my over-sensitivity kicks in, grace erodes and I'm likely to revert to them. "All of me, good and bad" is the realization and acceptance that I am human and fallible, that it can take years of practice for a new behaviour to even have a chance of becoming my new default setting. That is real humility.

I have to trust that I'm on the right path, that I'll be okay, and ask that I be granted ". . . the strength, as I go out from here, to do your bidding." It's really hard to practice being open and honest, or sometimes to just shut up! I sometimes have to hit this "reset button" many times a day. Ugh. Thy will, not mine, be done. Make me an instrument of your peace.

Step 8

Made a list of all persons we had harmed, and became willing to make amends to them all.

Getting Ready for Freedom

Conrod F. (Punanai 2012)

By the time I reached the doors of AA, my alcoholism, coupled with my addiction, was full-blown. My lies, manipulations, resentments and inner anger had left a trail of broken friendships, broken promises, heartbreak, tears and debts that were not going to go away just because I had decided to get sober.

The Promises tell us:

> "If we are painstaking about this phase of our development we will be amazed before we are half way through. We are going to know a new freedom and a new happiness. We will not regret the past nor wish to shut the door on it. We will comprehend the word serenity and we will know peace."

I had heard these words read a thousand times at meetings and I wanted them for myself. I had seen others who in my mind had achieved this state of being; if AA and the Steps gave it to them, then bring it on. After all, freedom and happiness were what I had always been chasing — in fact, they're what alcohol had promised way back in the early days of my drinking.

And to think that there could be a day when I would not regret my past after years of trying to use booze and drugs to stuff it away in a faraway room and shut the door — well, this was worth the effort. The earlier Steps had already given me faith in the program and in my sponsor and had, better yet, introduced me to a faith in God that proved over and over that fear was of no use and that faith was the way of my journey.

So, fearlessly, with the guidance of my sponsor, I set out on Step Eight.

The first thing I had to learn was that amends were entirely different from apologies. An amends has to do with restoring justice as much

97

as possible, to restore that which we have broken or damaged or to make restoration with some form of symbolic gesture, directly or indirectly.

I must admit that this was a foreign concept to me. For a very long time, my routine had been to try to avoid as much as possible those I had wronged — and especially those I had owed. And if I could not avoid them, then I had responded with anger or complete denial that a wrong had ever been committed. In a few extreme cases, when it was to my benefit, an apology coupled with a sob story was sometimes mustered up to temporarily save face or to ensure that my drinking or drugging was not impeded, but almost never had I made right a wrong.

I found that making the list was fairly easy, since I had already made a good start during and after the completion of my personal housekeeping in Step Four. After a few additions that came from further clarity and from the continued lifting of the fog that had clouded my memory in early sobriety, I was now armed with what I needed for my Step Nine.

I set off imagining how and when and where these great amends would happen; the beautiful outcome of most and the disastrous outcome of others. I shared my great imagination with my sponsor, who abruptly reminded me that I was on Step Eight, not Step Nine, and that my job at this stage was to become willing.

So off to the dictionary I was sent to refocus on the meaning of willingness. The first definition I came across was this: "the quality or state of being prepared to do something; readiness." After talking again to my sponsor, I knew that to get myself to a state of readiness, I needed to be okay with each and every amends I would make. I could not set out on an amends with any residue of resentment or fear, and I could not have any expectations of outcomes.

This would prove more difficult than anticipated, because there were still some people and institutions on that list that I truly did not feel ready to confront. Again, the lessons of my program came to my aid. I choose the names I would start with; those most important to my day-to-day living and that were essential for me to move forward. "First things first."

Then I began to pray on each one, asking for strength and courage, and often praying for the person — asking for them all that I would have for myself. Slowly, the fear and any remaining hesitation subsided and I reached a state of readiness — almost confidence — in what was about to come in my Step Nine.

If I move along my spiritual journey in sobriety without making an attempt to stand and rectify the wrongs of my past, I will have left areas where I will certainly meet resistance and therefore may ultimately seek to avoid them. The Twelve Promises suggest freedom — and true freedom means I must be rid of these barriers. Step Eight is when I set out to list those barriers and reach a state of readiness and willingness to restore justice to the best of my ability.

I am truly amazed and blessed to have been given an opportunity to ready myself for the glorious freedom that the preparation of Step Eight led me to in the remaining Steps.

Cleaning House

Cici C.

Hello, my name is Cici C. and I am a recovered alcoholic and by recovered I mean that the obsession has been lifted by working all Twelve Steps, continuously!

I had my last drink on February 29, 2008 and a week later went to a treatment "spa." I was told I would rest, eat well, do some yoga and have time to journal at this place. About 10 days in, "I came to" and had a panic attack. I had come to this place because I was powerless and I needed a rest. I recognized that I was sick and needed help from others; a Power greater than myself. I was told I would need this Power every day for the rest of my life to prevent the soul sickness from coming back.

I had always been a spiritual and religious person; however, in my sickness, I had been convinced that God was my only friend in the world and that he was done with me. It was easy for me to return to a daily ritual of prayer. But they also spoke of cleaning house . . .

Once I left the spa, I decided to attend AA meetings a couple of times a week, just in case what I had been told was true. During my first few months, I would ask approachable, sane-looking people, "What does it mean to do the work, to do the Steps?" They would start telling me about sponsors and I would smile politely, say thank you and walk away. I didn't need help reading a book! It took about nine months of observation — actually, nine months of loneliness and emotional instability — before I decided to ask for the help of a sponsor and start doing this work.

Every Step is important, and Step Eight appeared to be relatively easy. Make a list and be willing!

As my sponsor directed, I began my Step Eight list by looking at my Step Four list and reviewing it for people I had harmed. My list wasn't very long — my immediate family, close friends, my employer and a couple of ex-boyfriends. A few times, she asked me who I'd left off the list and would stare at me pointedly.

As we reviewed it, she gave me examples from the Big Book of the different types of amends, such as living amends, letters to deceased loved ones, financial amends, institutional amends and, of course, direct amends.

My sponsor gave me a formula, again from the Big Book, for scripting the amend: *I was selfish ... I was dishonest ... I hurt you by acting this way ... I deeply regret these behaviours, and by using the principles of the program, I will be a better daughter/sister/friend/ employee ... Have I left anything out?*

This all seemed very straightforward and I knew that it would be difficult for me but I was willing and I wanted desperately to walk in the Sunlight of the Spirit.

What surprised me was that we ended up crossing two names off the list! When my sponsor asked how I had hurt these two people, I didn't have an answer. They were on my list because I had believed for years that they had hurt me, even though I had walked away from them, quietly praying that they would suffer terrible diseases. Again she asked, how did I hurt them? Metaphysically! As I became frustrated, we went back to my Step Four list, specifically column four and my character defects: pride and self-pity.

Suddenly it became clear. These two ex-boyfriends were on my list because I had allowed them to rent space in my head and direct my future relationships for the next 20 years. Over the years, I had expended a lot of time and energy telling myself how they had wronged me and, in doing so, I had allowed them to continue hurting me, or so I believed. It was self-pity that allowed me to continually play the martyr in intimate relationships. I didn't owe them any amends! I was using that story to play the victim. I was harming myself.

I'd left *myself* off my Step Eight list. I owed myself an amend, and that amend was forgiveness. This was a small part of cleaning house!

Becoming Willing

Dave M. (Sullivan 2005)

One of the smartest things about the Twelve Steps of Alcoholics Anonymous is that Bill and Bob put a preparation Step before each action Step. Step Eight prepared me for the action of making amends in Step Nine.

Step Eight reads, "Made a list of all persons we had harmed, and became willing to make amends to them all." The key words for me in this Step are *became willing*. The willingness that I first had to become sober had to be carried into this Step. I had to become willing to make amends to the people and institutions I had harmed while drinking and drugging.

The list for Step Eight came out of my Step Four. I divided the list into three categories:

- Those I could make amends to right away

- Those I wasn't sure if I could make amends to

- Those I thought I *never* would be able to make amends to

Once the list was broken up, I was on my way. It was easy to finish Part One, and once I finished making those amends, I found it easy to move on to Part Two. Then it was time to tackle Part Three. By the time I got this far, I found it easy to tackle the majority of names, but some names took a few years.

If the willingness had not yet come or I was unable to find some people on my list, I did not let that deter me from moving on through the rest of the Steps, coming back to Steps Eight and Nine when my Higher Power's will allowed me to do so.

One of the most common mistakes people make while in or just coming out of treatment is to skip from one of the early Steps directly to Step Eight. This can be very dangerous. When I made this mistake, I found that I wasn't prepared for a person on my list to not care if I made amends or not, or that I was trying to straighten out my life. By not waiting to finish the middle Steps, I had not prepared myself emotionally or spiritually to accept rejection. Luckily, I had a good sponsor who talked me through it and pointed out the error of my ways. By skipping ahead without being prepared, I put my sobriety in danger. This is why the old timers tell us never to skip Steps and to do them in the order the founders wrote them.

Sometimes a name is not on our list. When I first did the Steps, I was still foggy and couldn't remember everything from my past. I knew that the Steps were important, though, and that I had to start them right away to ensure that my personal growth did not stagnate.

One day as I was backing out of my driveway, I saw a long-lost friend pulling out of his driveway. It hit me immediately that, although he wasn't on my amends list, I owed this person a direct amends. I quickly drove my car into his driveway and blocked him in. Jumping out of my car, I went up to his vehicle and immediately told him that I owed him an amends and why. He declared that I didn't owe him anything, but I said it was actually for me and not for him, and that if I did not do this, it would endanger my sobriety. As part of the amends, I explained the changes that had occurred in my life and my goals for sobriety. My friend was quite happy for me and we parted on good terms.

It is always important to remember that an amends is not just saying "sorry." The definition of amends is "to compensate for loss or damage." In many cases, "sorry" didn't cut it. Money had to be paid back.

In the case of my father, I had to make a living amends. He had heard "sorry" too many times to count. I had to walk the AA talk and not just provide lip service. During my first year, I came home every night before 11:00 p.m. so he didn't have to go to bed worrying about me. I kept my word and began to straighten out my career. By the fourth year of sobriety, I was honoured to take care of him after he was hit by a major stroke, until he died a few months later.

The power of Alcoholics Anonymous and Step Eight show that a former active alcoholic and addict, a former liar, cheat and thief can redeem himself, turn things around and be responsible enough to care for a dying family member. Living amends allowed me to be there for my father without him or other family members having to worry that I would screw things up by going on a bender.

As I finished Step Eight and neared the end of Step Nine, the Twelve Promises began to come to fruition, just as the Big Book promised me they would. By becoming willing to make amends, I had added to the daily reprieve my Higher Power gives me to stay away from that first drink.

Step 9

Made direct amends to such
people wherever possible, except
when to do so would injure them
or others.

At the Right Time, With the Right Intentions

Susan M. (Munro 2010)

When I first sobered up, I thought that I could just run around and say I was sorry and all would be right with the world. I could just point out all the things that had been done to me and then say sorry for reacting the way I did. Everyone would forgive me because I was so special — the towering ego!

Luckily for me, I found guidance in my sponsor, Peggy. She walked me through the first eight Steps at the perfect pace. Steps One through Eight prepared me for some of the toughest things I've ever had to do. I had to acknowledge to those I had hurt that I was in fact responsible for my feelings and actions. I had to accept that there may not be forgiveness by the person. In some cases, the amends could never directly happen. And I had thought just not drinking was hard!

Step Nine states, "Made direct amends to such people whenever possible, except when to do so would injure them or others." When I first read this Step, I could see the "escape clause": the part that says except when to do so would injure them or others. So if I wasn't comfortable making the amends, wasn't that going to further injure me? Clearly, I was still a little self-centred when I first came into the program.

Working with my sponsor, asking questions and attending meetings slowly worked to change my perspective on things. Where once I saw the "escape clause" as pertaining to me, I now see it really refers to the ones that I have hurt.

Step Nine is not about absolution or blame. It is to acknowledge my actions; my part in things. This is another step forward in my recovery, in my healing and in my spiritual growth. By taking it slowly, I was able to work on Step Nine in such a way that I found great relief in my very soul for past mistakes. I found forgiveness, love and compassion in areas where there had been only anger, hurt and envy.

For me, there are three different types of amends that I need to make in order to stay sober: direct, indirect and living. I must carefully consider each person who is owed amends. What is my motivation behind it? Am I considering the other person? Or am I being selfish?

Direct amends must be done at the right time, with the right intentions. When I sit down with someone, it cannot be because I am looking for that person's forgiveness. I am not there to argue or place blame. While forgiveness would be great, it is okay if that person is unable to do so. I ask only for a little time, patience and understanding. There can be no expectation of what is going to happen, for expectations can become resentments very quickly. And resentments will surely kill me.

In preparing for my direct amends, my sponsor advised me to write down what I wanted to say. I reviewed my Fourth Step involving the individual. I reflected on it, prayed for guidance and started to write. And as I wrote, any remaining anger and resentments were lifted from me. I was looking only at my inventory, my part in everything that had happened. I was the one who was selfish, self-seeking and had tried in vain to force things to be the way I thought they should be. In acknowledging my character defects, I found forgiveness for myself.

Indirect amends are the ones I do for the people I would further injure by making direct amends. Or for those who had been hurt as a third or fourth party because of my actions. Do I make direct amends with the ex-wife of a guy I had an affair with? Am I concerned with what effect it would have on her? Will she be further hurt? Or am I trying only to appease myself? These amends are done between me and the God of my understanding. I ask his forgiveness for my actions. And I pray that the person involved may have found happiness in his or her life.

Living amends started the day I decided to do something about my alcoholism. Each day since June 1, 2011, I have stayed sober. I have lived the Twelve Principles of the AA program to the best of my abilities — the principles that have taught me honesty, compassion, love and understanding. Today, I try to do the next right thing. I try to be the best person I know how to be. This is my living amends to my children, family, friends and even my employer. For me, saying sorry isn't enough. I have to live it.

The Jewellery Box

Joshua H.

I call my mother's mother Grammy. I'm still not sure what her real name is, and I've always felt too embarrassed to ask any of my siblings if they know her full name (which I'm quite confident they do). It's entirely possible that her name is Abby, but I've questioned whether that's a false assumption pulled from the remnants of memories from my Grammy's bathroom.

Her bathroom smelled strongly of rosehip soap and baby powder. It wasn't an altogether unpleasant smell, but something about its indistinct antiquity made me a bit uncomfortable. As a little guy, I was fascinated by the many containers that held secret things old ladies used to make themselves smell and appear younger.

I liked her collection of magazines and Sears catalogues, which afforded me my first glimpses of mature women posing unflinchingly in their underwear. I was also compulsively drawn to reading advice columns.

I felt a voyeuristic thrill in reading about the problems of adults. I liked that at times adults came upon situations so baffling to them that they needed the intervention of this woman Abby. She seemed to possess information ranging from the exact temperature required to cook the perfect turkey to whether or not your husband was sleeping with the neighbour's wife.

To me, Abby represented a sense of order in what I was already beginning to suspect was a chaotic world. So, I admit it's quite possible my Grammy's real name was not actually Abby.

Grammy doted on me. I was little, cute and apparently funny. She liked to drive me around in her Ford Country Squire station wagon and regale me with stories of her childhood. I remember the pleasantness of her voice as we drove with the back window rolled partially down, me standing on the back bench seat facing out the window with my small hands clasped over the top of the wind-cooled glass.

I don't have a lot of childhood memories — at a later age, I unwittingly traded in a great many of them to recreationally sniff airplane glue. But every so often, especially in the fall, I'll catch a faint breeze off the open window of my car that jars loose those particular memories, and I'll hear that pleasant whisper describing life on Locust Street.

In the early 1990s, after I had blown all of my money on a potentially suicidal intake of heroin and crack cocaine, I found myself standing in the bedroom of the house with the rosehip-smelling bathroom. I stared in the vanity mirror atop the dresser and saw my own wild, frantic eyes looking back at me. Abby sat silently in her front living room waiting for my uncle to arrive so he could escort me out of the city where I had grown up.

I had developed a tremor in my hands, partly from the drug withdrawal I was experiencing, but perhaps more from the disgust I had for what I was about to do. I remember lifting the cool ceramic lid covering the contents of the jewellery box, and the imperceptible "don't" that I whispered to myself before my hand closed over the crumpled $20 bills inside. I furtively hid them in my pocket.

I pretended to come out of the bathroom so she wouldn't know I had been in her bedroom, and I sat in silence in the living room until my uncle arrived. I knew when I walked out that door, unable to look her in the eyes, that she knew I'd been in her bedroom. Any remaining bit of dignity I'd possessed had been abandoned in her heavy old jewellery box.

Shortly after, I sat across from my uncle in a diner that stank of stale coffee, cigarettes and despair. He quietly placed a small sum of cash on the table, cleared his throat and informed me that I would not be welcomed back by any of my relatives until I had gotten help. None of them wanted to watch me kill myself, especially not Grammy, he said. Before I took the money, I had to agree to not come home.

I agreed, and did not return until I had been clean and sober for several years.

The passage of time is often unkind. Grammy began to show early signs of dementia. My mother called me last December to tell me the doctors did not expect Grammy would live much past Christmas. The slight strain of sadness in my mother's voice reminded me that she was not just talking about my Grammy, but also about her own mother. Before hanging up, she asked me to think of something I'd shared with Grammy, just her and I.

This is what I thought:

In the late 1990s on a fall afternoon, I stood outside a church for my sister's wedding. I was wearing a suit. Grammy tearfully told me she had hardly even recognized me; that I had grown into a handsome gentleman.

After we hugged, I folded my hand over the open palm of her wrinkled hand and pressed several crumpled $20 bills into it. I closed her hand over the bills, and before she could protest. I shook my head and said, "Please ... for me."

For a moment, she stood perfectly still, then nodded, and in quiet acknowledgment closed her hand, knowing exactly how much money I had given her, and knowing exactly what she was allowing me to buy back.

A New Freedom

Bridget J. (Munro 2004)

In the 2007 film *You Kill Me*, Ben Kingsley's character is a recovering alcoholic and a professional hit man. The movie depicts him making his amends by sending Sony gift cards to the families of his victims. Courageous? Indeed. Using good judgment? Well, it is a comedy after all. I can't help thinking about how easy it would be to make amends like that in the real world.

Before embarking on making amends, I practice Step Eight as a way to end being alone, to lose fear of my fellows and to improve my connection with God. Step Eight helps me become willing to make further changes by listing my mistakes and harms to others.

When carrying out Step Nine, I need to carefully consider those I have harmed and reflect upon each situation before directly admitting the damage I caused — whether it was to an employer (current or past), a family member, a friend or anyone else I have wronged.

There are those, too, who have been on the receiving end of an amend who did not make it onto my grudge list when I did a Fourth Step inventory. I also have to remember the second part of Step Nine, which states "except when to do so would injure them or others." This includes me.

When it comes to a deep-seated hurt that I am responsible for and when the amend must be done face to face, I first make a point to review it with my sponsor or someone who understands and respects the 12-step program. Praying to God and asking for His help and guidance truly helps to give me the courage and strength to carry out what I must do in order to stay sober and serene, no matter what the outcome will be.

God has a wonderful way of putting people in my path when I least expect it. One example that comes to mind happened after being sober for a couple of years. Upon exiting a Joe and Charlie Big Book

Study, I saw an old roommate, one who had moved out on account of my very strange behaviour that was associated with my excessive drinking at the time. I took a moment to pray, then approached her and asked if she had a few minutes to talk. (I, of course, wanted to admit my faults from years previous and make amends.) Her answer was "No, I don't have time, I have to leave." I had to accept that perhaps another chance would happen for me to clear the wreckage of the past situation with this person. It also indicated to me that I needed to let go of the fear relating to predicting an outcome.

This past week, after admitting my faults and attempting to clear away some wreckage with someone, I was told off and criticized. I must admit that I felt worse than before asking to meet with the person. As difficult as it was to sit there while being judged and criticized, I humbly listened to what the other person had to say, without any reaction, waited for them to finish talking, then told them that what I needed to say had been said and thanked them for their time. It was a good reminder to me that how another person reacts to an amends is none of my business.

I have also been on the receiving end of attitudes like, "Oh, whatever. No problem." Sometimes it's good, sometimes not. Keeping it simple and direct helps me to stay on track and not lose focus on what I honestly need to talk about.

I have the chance daily to make a different kind of amend: a living amend. To me, a living amend helps me to be of service to the world I live in, outside of the confines of AA meetings, where effort and willingness help to connect me with others.

The focus of Step Nine, for me, is self-discipline. It is more than saying "I am sorry." It has nothing to do with asking for or wanting forgiveness, either. It has freed me from the obstacles of my past mistakes in a miraculous way.

My life has changed and continues to change. I have opportunities now to mend fences instead of burn bridges, and when the ill will that poisoned me for years is washed away, existence becomes peaceful. If I am honest about the amends I make and work Step Nine as long as I must, I will truly know a new freedom and a new happiness.

Step 10

Continued to take personal inventory and when we were wrong promptly admitted it.

Today I Ask Myself . . .

Karen B. (Munro 2012)

I have a deep affection for Step Ten. For me, it is putting out the garbage every day and returning to kind and thoughtful thinking. I plan my morning and ask for my higher power's help and guidance for the day. I feel a sense of calm and focus wash over me.

A favourite quote and cornerstone of following the practice of Step Ten is on page 88 of the *Twelve and Twelve*: "Can we stay sober, keep in emotional balance, and live to good purpose under all conditions?" If I ask myself these questions, I immediately find out if I am on or off the beam.

When I find myself getting caught up in negative thinking, I journal about it. Writing my thoughts down brings to light some answers that I believe I couldn't have come to otherwise. If I'm not paying attention to what is coming up for me each day, I won't know how to deal with the problem, or even that there is a problem at all. I am reminded of my reoccurring character defects and that, indeed, they need to be addressed. After working the previous nine Steps, this doesn't induce guilt or shame as it once did. It's like a light bulb switching on, so that I can be aware of it and make progress.

An important issue that keeps coming up for me while working Step Ten is confronting head-on what I feel is justifiable anger. If something or someone upsets me, what is wrong with me that makes me feel this way? I prefer to own this emotion since I have no control over the thoughts and feelings of anyone else.

I have learned that anger is dangerous no matter what the cause and I need to keep my side of the street clean. Sometimes that involves an apology. Sometimes it means that I need to forgive or let go. But I certainly know that I am a lot sicker when I hold on to it. If I'm aware, it doesn't need to turn into a deep resentment. I don't feel the need to lash out or gossip. I catch my motives before taking action.

When I was using, I acted very impulsively, not thinking before I spoke. I often demanded my own way whether it was reasonable or not. Step Ten teaches me to take a step back and give myself a chance to act with care and love. And when I don't catch it in the moment and I badly act out, I can identify that an amend needs to be made. It gives me the opportunity to change my behaviour before it turns into a damaged relationship or a misunderstanding.

I believe that all the important relationships in my life have benefited from working Step Ten. I don't need to make the same mistakes and it keeps me honest and humble. I am also much more at peace in my life if I'm not holding on to needless negative thoughts and feelings. My higher power alerts me to needed revisions to my attitude, when I take the time to investigate my actions for the day. The process of this daily spot check and inventory is as important as house cleaning to me; as important as getting the laundry or dishes done every day.

So today I ask myself ... Can I stay sober? Yes! Keep in emotional balance? Yes! One day at a time! And live to good purpose under all conditions? With the help of Step Ten, I'm making progress ... not perfection.

The "24-hour" Rule

Terry G. (Munro 1997)

Nobody likes to admit to being wrong. But it is absolutely necessary for me to maintain spiritual progress in my recovery.

It is a process which seems on the surface to be difficult to face, but in actuality it is as much a benefit to the one admitting the wrong as it is to the person who was wronged. By promptly facing mistakes and taking responsibility for them, it prevents situations from festering into resentments and anger that can become real problems.

This Step was not easy for me in the beginning. When I worked the Twelve Steps the first time, I still held some resentments. I truly believe that these Steps need be done over and over again for this very reason. Step Ten is one of the three "maintenance Steps," which come easier for me as time passes and my head clears more and more with each new day.

I've done lots of challenging work as I've gone through the Steps so far. As much as I might want to slow down, relax, or even stop, I need to be careful about sliding back into old habits and patterns.

I find today that in practicing a daily check-in, the observation and self-reflection monitor my life in a spiritual way and maintain the progress I have already made. I can pinpoint something I've done wrong and clear it up as fast as I can — the same day or the next day.

In early sobriety, I still had anger issues, so I gave myself a "24-hour" rule. If I was angered or bothered by something or someone, I would wait until I could review the situation and not say something I would regret later. Believe it or not, I wasn't angry or troubled by the next day and would make the amends. If it was something out of my control, like something that happened at work, I would speak to the appropriate people the next day to have the air cleared.

When I get a daily check-up in Step Ten, I discover where my mind needs emotional and spiritual health, just the same as a physical check-up. Step Ten helps to keep my spiritual house clean. All humans are bound to make mistakes and errors. Owning up to these wrongs quickly settles the issue. Rather than weighing on my conscience or building up to produce greater consequences, the mistake is corrected promptly and the problem nipped in the bud.

AA has given me a "daily reprieve" from my drinking as long as I continue to practice what I have learned so far in my recovery. I have taken the Steps to understand my past and have taken full responsibility for myself. Now I apply what I have learned to the present.

Today, I have realized that whatever happens to me emotionally, spiritually or even physically allows me to grow, with a new attitude and build character every day. Without mistakes in life, I would have never changed. I can now look forward to every day as an opportunity to make changes happen.

Balancing My Emotional Ledger

Anne P. (Munro 2005)

It didn't seem like such a bad idea to take a vacation during my first year of recovery. For New Year's. With a non-alcoholic girlfriend. To an all-inclusive.

I had some savings (all the money I hadn't been spending on you-know-what) and I didn't think it was necessary for my sponsor to weigh in on this decision so ... off I went.

In favour of my sobriety was the fact that my travelling companion didn't really care whether she drank or not (yes, those people exist) and so she made a commitment to also avoid alcohol. We agreed to indulge ourselves in the other vices that had become the rituals of our relationship: drinking coffee, eating chocolate and smoking cigarettes. Also helpful was that our hotel was situated in a very old city, so there was an abundance of interesting things to see and do.

At the hotel's restaurant, our servers got to know us the way servers do when you stay somewhere for a few days and follow a certain schedule. When we arrived at dinnertime, for example, our drinks were waiting for us — virgin pina coladas. They were heavenly. Freshly squeezed pineapple juice, freshly crushed coconut, creamy and sweet.

One evening, later in our stay, we turned up for dinner to find a different server. Fine. We ordered our drinks, sure to emphasize *bebida virgin* and *sin alcohol*. It seemed as though he understood. When our drinks arrived, I took a gulp through the straw and immediately felt the fire scorching my tongue and burning its way down my throat. My girlfriend watched me as I started to shake and my eyes welled up with tears. I felt as though I had just failed. Everything.

My friend snatched up our drinks and stormed over to the bartender. She reminded him angrily that we had never ordered alcohol and asked why he hadn't recognized us. The staff were apologetic and perplexed. She gave up on them and came back to our table, gave me a hug and asked what I needed to do. I said, "I need to go to a meeting." She took me by the arm and led me back to our room. I asked her if she would read the *Twelve and Twelve* with me. She said she'd love to. I asked for her favourite number between one and 12. She said 10. So we read Step Ten.

She had attended a few meetings with me. She had respect for Alcoholics Anonymous and could see how well it worked in peoples' lives, but she had never read the Steps or really given them much thought. After we had finished reading the Step together, in between puffs of our cigarettes, slurps of coffee and, of course, bites of chocolate, she looked at me in amazement. "This Step is a recipe for living," she said. "It isn't about being an alcoholic; it's about being happy." We read more together and even got into the Big Book and some of the stories at the back. Late into the night, we talked and read and puffed and sipped and nibbled.

The next day was New Year's Eve. I felt a huge sense of relief, strength and humility. Bringing in the new year was spectacular. From the wall of an ancient fortress, we watched fireworks over the ocean in front of a full, clear moon. Then we retreated to our hotel room for another "meeting" and the beginnings of what would become a daily routine of taking inventory and balancing my emotional ledger.

Step Ten reminds us to maintain balance and stay alert to the daily disturbances that, left unchecked and unexamined, can so quickly drag us back down the path of misery. "Step back and think," it tells us. Good advice, which I have since heeded with respect to maintaining my sobriety, among many other things.

Now, in my daily life as a mother, Step Ten has a significant relevance. Children under the age of five are sort of like little alcoholics, aren't they? Self-centred, quick-tempered and emotionally unbalanced, they waver back and forth in an instant from arrogant pride to debilitating fear and disappointment. "It is pointless to become angry, or to get hurt by people who, like us, are suffering from the pains of growing up." Hmmm. Children provide an excellent opportunity to practice self-restraint and to begin to "approach true tolerance and see what real love for our fellows actually means."

"Courtesy, kindness, justice, and love" are critical attributes with which to treat others and be treated, but also to generate within our children. These are qualities that can be learned only by example, by watching them at work, by knowing what they feel like. My progress, certainly not any perfection, will hopefully serve as one of the greatest gifts I can give my kids.

Step 11

Sought through prayer and meditation to improve our conscious contact with God *as we understood Him*, praying only for knowledge of His will for us and the power to carry that out.

Conscious Continuous Contact — Expect Miracles!

Christopher C.

When I received my one-year medallion, two people instrumental in my recovery each gave me a card on which they wrote messages I will never forget. Joan, over 25 years sober, simply wrote "Keep up the good work." Betty, over 30 years sober and my chosen speaker that night, wrote "Steps Three and Eleven are where the miracles are."

"Keep up the good work." It meant to me that I must have been doing something right — I was sober after all! However, it also meant don't rest on my laurels for too long, keep up the good effort, keep seeking.

"Steps Three and Eleven are where the miracles are." This told me my relationship with my Higher Power is of utmost importance if I want to stay serene. I am at great risk of relapse when I am restless, irritable and discontent. The way to stay free is by turning my life and will over to my Higher Power and seeking this through prayer and meditation. Step Eleven helps me keep conscious contact. It is an active process. Betty said that I could expect miracles if I did this.

A definition I found from the playwright George Bernard Shaw makes sense:

> "Miracles, in the sense of phenomena we cannot explain, surround us on every hand: life itself is the miracle of miracles."

For this alcoholic, life is miraculous. When I drank, I was doing the miracle of life a disservice. I was doing my life a grave injustice. No more — I am sober now.

Eventually I replaced the words "Him" and "God" in Step Eleven with "Higher Power." I feel there is no way God can be just a he or a she. The Higher Power I seek through prayer and meditation is too big to be one thing, is immense, is everything one can imagine, think and experience. Really, it is indefinable — but findable. God is perhaps the most loaded three-letter word we have, no doubt due to all the horrendous acts that have been committed in that name. As a former atheist, it took me a long while to come to terms with the word God. I find "Higher Power" less loaded; it has zero negative connotations when pondering spiritual matters with self and others.

When I came into recovery, there was so much that was negative in my world view, I needed something more powerful than my dis-ease that was positive and would put me at ease. I needed a HP that was kind, gentle and loving, to be that way with others and myself; something that would empower me to move forward, to heal and to recover from a hopeless state of mind and body. What kind of power could do this?

Someone said God is love, and love is God. I thought, *Now, love is a Higher Power I can trust.* For it was in the 12-step rooms that I was restored to sanity and unconditionally loved back to health. The program and the people in it were GOD — "Group of Drunks" — and the Twelve Steps my "Good Orderly Direction." An atheist I knew who died 30 years sober told me that he got sober by associating with recovering people. That was a power greater than him. These were simple, profound and practical words. So I began in this way.

Prayer and meditation helped me to touch and maintain peace of mind; something I had very little of while drinking and drugging. I don't have to believe in anything to meditate — simply practice and see what happens. It brought me faith from direct experience as I found peace, joy and calm just below the surface of fear, anxiety and depression. I am learning to face and embrace life's challenges. When I open my eyes in the morning, I no longer dread the day to come. I sit up in bed, say a prayer (talking to HP) and meditate (listening to HP). Sometimes, I become absorbed in meditation and forget myself. How wonderful! The self-will disappears. Meditation has become a rich part of my life.

Magnetic resonance imaging taken of the brains of advanced meditation practitioners shows that the areas of the brain that correspond to joy, happiness, well-being and resilience light up while they meditate. In fact, one advanced meditation practitioner lit up the instruments so much that the researchers thought the machine wasn't working properly! They asked him to stop, checked their machine, had him start again and got the same results. So on the biological or physical level, the constant, gentle, loving, ongoing practice of meditation literally changes the brain neurologically and chemically. We can awaken to a new consciousness.

Whenever I ask recovering people why they do not meditate, the answers are usually different ways of saying, "I just don't make the time for it." A wise man once said, "The proof of the pudding is in the eating." So to benefit, I must partake in it. The ongoing practice of prayer and meditation has changed my mind, body and spirit in ways I never imagined. My life is delicious and yours can be too!

Finally, Step Eleven says, "praying only for knowledge of His will for us." What then is God's will? It can sound kind of ominous at first. But I've learned it's simple. It is everything I experience in my life moment to moment. *All* of it: the good, the bad, the beautiful, the ugly, the tedious, boring, exciting, loving, hating, happy, joyful, sorrowful, tearful, peaceful, angry; no exceptions, life in totality. I am learning to accept whatever happens without grasping and without aversion. I know that by maintaining contact, I am empowered to live this life fully, sanely and soberly.

I find it best expressed in a succinct saying I found from the ancient Bon tradition of Tibet, who have some of the most beautiful and direct spiritual writings and meditations. Their view and mine can best be summed up like this: neither accepting nor rejecting, but leaving everything just as it is and that is good. When I do this, there is no problem.

Julian of Norwich explains the fruit of practice: "All shall be well, and all shall be well, and all manner of things shall be well."

My view of life has completely changed in recovery due to prayer and meditation. It gives me peace of mind and empowers me to live happily, asking only for the wisdom to know the meaning of this life and being empowered to live it one day at a time. In the beginning, I prayed to stop drinking and my prayer was answered. That was miraculous enough. Yet, I was freely given so much more by seeking to improve my spiritual contact. It is miraculous to be on this journey. I am a most fortunate and grateful person.

The end of the Serenity Prayer, seldom said, is, "Thy will, not mine, be done." This means accept life on life's terms, and it's a miraculous fruit of the program. May you become happy and free from suffering on your recovery journey and be empowered to serenely accept all you experience!

Learning to Listen

Louise S. (Family Program)

Step Eleven is the bedrock of my 12-step programs. It reminds me that I have a Higher Power to whom I can turn for guidance at any moment of the day. Over many years, I have learned to trust that I am being guided and protected in all my actions and that every situation is a learning opportunity.

My upbringing was in a religious household where evening prayers and weekly services were the norm. I was told what was expected of me and I complied. My concept of a Higher Power was that he was benevolent, but certainly expected the rules to be followed. If they weren't, atonement had to be made.

Learning to reach a place of trust took a long time and I still have temporary struggles with it. The idea of praying for knowledge of God's will for me was something I had never heard of, and trusting that God would know what was best for me was too big a leap of faith. How could I trust that God would listen and would know what was best for me?

Friends told me to "act as if" and when I did, it worked. I was shocked, surprised and delighted. It was as if a different person was inhabiting my body and acting in a way that was far more God-centred and peaceful than I could have done on my own. I was gaining insight as to how this all worked.

Step Eleven offers me a solution: prayer and meditation. These two tools are important resources through which I can experience God's guidance — and be still so I can hear it.

I begin every day by praying for guidance throughout the day and the willingness to carry that out. I also pray for a day that is productive, joyful and nurturing. Throughout the day when faced with indecision, I pray for the right choice to be louder. When stuck in a difficult situation, I ask God what He would have me do to take the next right step. These sorts of prayers help me to gain clarity and I am then better able to move forward peacefully.

After prayer, I often make a to-do list and then turn this list over to my Higher Power. At the end of the day, I may have accomplished some or all of the things on that list. The important thing for me is that I have given the list to God and have listened to my intuition of where to begin and where to stop. When I take this action, I can relax and let the day unfold peacefully.

By practising Step Eleven, I know that with my Higher Power's guidance, whatever I do during the day is enough. I can let go of thinking that I need to be superhuman and simply accept that I am good enough, no matter what gets done.

My spiritual practice includes daily readings. It may also include the AA *Twelve and Twelve*, the Big Book and other literature relating to my different programs. Afterwards, I journal. I find this tool particularly helpful as it lets me put on the page all the thoughts that are rumbling around in my brain and allows me to write out any decisions I need help in solving.

I finish with meditation, which I find especially nurturing. I do it as frequently as I can. I always feel better afterwards but like many things that are good for me, I have some resistance. I began by joining a meditation group, which was very spiritually and emotionally enriching. I followed through by practising on my own.

When I don't feel I can sit in silence, I listen to a guided meditation. Both types help me to be still and focus on my breathing. Meditation brings me in touch with staying in the moment and the knowledge that life is unfolding exactly as it should.

When I take the time to pause and connect with my Higher Power through prayer and meditation, I can move forward with more clarity and peace. It is through the practising of Step Eleven that I continue to gain more trust in "His will for [me] and the power to carry that out." I am learning that it is not up to me to make the world unfold, and I find more peace and serenity when I accept that things are as they should be. I need to do nothing but listen.

An Unshakeable Foundation for Life

Charles M. (Punanai 2001)

"Life is difficult."

So begins *The Road Less Traveled*, a wisdom book about living well by M. Scott Peck. Talk about keeping it simple! We hear the same awareness time and again in the rooms of recovery: "Just because I'm sober doesn't mean my life is easy."

I had no idea what Peck was talking about when I first opened his book back in the mid-1980s — probably because I was neck deep in my addiction and desperate to believe that everything in my life would just work out. Magically.

Now I get it — probably because I've been clean and sober for awhile and I'm paying attention. Today, I'm free to say "yes" to life, and most days I choose to face life on *its* terms, not mine, as best I can.

Unfortunately for me, however, I don't always have answers for life's challenges. The next right action isn't always clear to me. In fact, living sober sometimes leaves me feeling as rudderless, scared and discouraged as I felt when I was using.

Life *is* difficult. And I don't mind admitting I need a power other than King "I" to help me live sober — just as I needed that same power to help me get sober.

Enter Step Eleven, my favourite Step.

Something about this Step grabbed me — I can't quite say what. I jumped right into it the day after I graduated from "The House." I still try my best to greet each new day with a time of prayerful and meditative quiet.

At first, this was new and it was hard. And I definitely still need discipline to keep it up. I do keep it up because I've grown to like how the still, deep quiet feeds my spirit. I need that. And I love the results.

Step Eleven is my anchor. Working this Step keeps me grounded in my relationship with the higher power I committed to in Step Three, and then some — it takes that relationship to a deeper place. I tap into courage when scared; strength when worn out; comfort when hurt or lonely; determination when discouraged. Step Eleven keeps me trudging along.

Over time, I've learned what works best for me. If I want solid results, I need a solid morning routine with built-in quality time for practicing the Step. A rush job doesn't cut it. For me, that's 20 minutes minimum — I prefer at least a half an hour, if not longer. And of course that dictates when I set the alarm!

I'm better at the conscious part of "conscious contact" if I start by taking what time I need to calm my thoughts, relax my body and settle into a true quiet. Sometimes that takes a few minutes and sometimes, on bad days, longer. And I'm more open — less easily distracted — if I do my Step work first thing in the morning, before the rush of getting ready for work.

Step Eleven is also my rudder. I can't describe how that works for me any better than the Step itself does:

> In thinking about our day we may face indecision. We may not be able to determine which course to take. Here we ask God for inspiration, an intuitive thought or a decision. We relax and take it easy. We don't struggle. We are often surprised how the right answers come . . .
> Alcoholics Anonymous, p. 86

"Ask." I don't always know what to do. When I was new and inexperienced with this Step, I'd pray for direction, then immediately look to the elders in recovery for advice. I still do.

"Relax and take it easy ... don't struggle." If I'm anxious and impatient, then I'm fighting the Step. That blocks the power in the process from doing *its* work.

And then, "Surprise!" A burden lifted; a door opened; a next step; a new direction.

Practicing this Step over time has given me a more open heart; one with a greater capacity to listen. It's more natural for me to sit and wait with patience. Best of all, I can better recognize the inspiration, or intuition, that actually does come from my deepest, truest self, from my wise child, from my God. And to trust it!

All in all, Step Eleven gives me an unshakeable foundation for life — just as it promised me.

Step 12

Having had a spiritual awakening as the result of these steps, we tried to carry this message to alcoholics, and to practice these principles in all our affairs.

An Expression of Who I've Become

JD M.

Early in my sobriety, I saw the Steps much like a ladder that I had to climb. Step Twelve was the last rung where I would get to ring the bell of recovery. Once I got there, my alcohol and drug problems would be behind me and life would be smooth sailing.

At early meetings, what I heard was that Step Twelve meant "service" and that I was expected to volunteer to do menial tasks like making coffee and setting up chairs. Later, I could graduate to administrative work like being group secretary. My pre-recovery experience told me that this was just another hazing process; a way for those who had been around for awhile to take advantage of me while laughing behind my back. I felt indignant. Don't you know who I am?

Well, I was desperate enough to stay clean and sober and to be accepted in the only place I felt somewhat safe, so I played along with my home group's regime. My first "volun-told" job was setting up chairs with two other guys — Darien, who was a newcomer like me, and Greg, who had about a year of sobriety and acted like he was our boss.

Darien and I had a laugh while we set up, telling jokes and swapping stories about odd people we had seen at meetings. We put up with Greg but didn't really include him in our conversations, because he was "management."

One week when Greg hadn't shown up on time, Darien and I decided to change the seating pattern from straight to curved rows, so all the seats were facing the podium. We were very proud of our initiative. However, when Greg arrived he blew a gasket and told us we had to put everything back the usual way. You can imagine how that made us feel about this service nonsense.

However, as time went on, Darien and I started to get a sense of it being *our* meeting, *our* group. Since we were always there early, we started to meet people — even some who thanked us for setting up!

And we started to recognize who was even newer than we were; people we could welcome to our home group. We were able to tell them how the meetings worked and what to expect. I could see the relief in their faces, realizing they had come to a safe place. What a good feeling.

After about a year, I had worked through the Steps with my sponsor as well as at several weekend Step studies, so I had a better knowledge of the program and felt I could pass on my experience, strength and hope to newcomers. I had developed a faith that the program worked for me. I kept thinking of that first line in Chapter Seven of the AA Big Book: "Practical experience shows that nothing will so much insure immunity from drinking as intensive work with other alcoholics."

So, with my sponsor's support, two significant things happened. First, I volunteered to answer the phones at the Intergroup office. Then, I got my first sponsee. I took my Step Twelve responsibilities seriously and found that doing this work gave me a deeper and more practical meaning to both the Fellowship and the Steps.

I was reminded to keep it simple. As a newcomer (and even now!), I was turned off by people giving me instructions, telling me what to do. My sponsor pointed out that the key is to offer friendship and fellowship (Big Book, page 95) and that it is my deportment (the way I conduct myself) and not what I say that is most convincing (Big Book, page 18).

As time went on, I found that my understanding of the Steps continued to change. Rather than a linear conception like a ladder with a bell at the top, I started to see it more like a pyramid with Step One as the foundation and the other Steps built on top. I came to see that Step One is really an understanding of who I am. I started to see the full extent of the unmanageability of life and my powerlessness over most of it. I started to see my sobriety as not just abstinence from my drug of choice (or no choice!) but as a place of emotional and mental sanity.

And, in the same way, I started to see Step Twelve not so much as the final task in my road to recovery, but rather as an expression of who I become as the result of the Steps. My responsibility was not only to pass the program on to others in the Fellowship but to practice the principles of the program (honesty, open-mindedness, willingness, etc.) in *all* my affairs. By practicing Steps One to Eleven, I become Step Twelve. And my effectiveness at that can wax and wane, depending on my maintaining a fit spiritual condition.

An Extraordinary Evolution

Shannon J. (Munro 1999)

Upon entering the program five years ago, my sponsor asked me a few simple questions, one of them being "once you have completed these Steps, are you willing to share your experience with others?" I remember distinctly scoffing and replying, "No one is going to want what I have." A dejected response from a very broken girl.

After four and a half years of blessed sobriety, my conceptions around the Twelfth Step have altered radically. I thought Step Twelve was all about sponsorship. However, I quite conveniently bypassed the second part, and for me, the most important aspect of Step Twelve: "practice[ing] these principles in all [my] affairs." Although sponsorship has been an amazing experience, it is in fact only half of this all-important Step. Sponsoring keeps my sobriety in check, but more importantly, it reminds me that in order to give something of value away, I have to practice a life of value.

The principles, for me, primarily consisted of honesty, open-mindedness and willingness, existing only in the realm of sobriety. At the time, that was all I was capable of looking at. These three principles took hold in varying degrees of success the more completely I decided to practice them. This happened for me in stages, but as I traversed my way through the Steps, other principles became apparent.

Surrendering to, conceptualizing, being guided by and maintaining a relationship with my Higher Power, whom I call God (Steps One, Two, Three and Eleven), was the barometer for how I conducted myself. Becoming unburdened by resentment, facing my fears, and accepting how they manifested in my behaviours and ultimately hurt the people I love (Steps Four, Five, Six, Seven and Eight), brought me clarity and presence of mind. It was within this clarity that the forgiveness of others (Step Nine) inspired me to begin that healing task of forgiving myself. This translated into the courage to take stock of myself daily, and set right any wrongs I had committed (Step Ten).

This way of living developed within me a moral compass and an unbelievable thing occurred. A life was being created.

With a tentative step, I went out into this newly created life. I began to learn about accountability and the importance of following through with what I said. I applied these new-found principles by enrolling in and completing my French degree: a dream of 22 years that finally came to fruition. I had finally finished something I started!

This built up my wavering self-esteem, and I took this blossoming confidence and volunteered my time with two organizations for which I had unbridled passion. The necessity of balance was at once introduced. I wanted to do it all perfectly, and wanted it completed yesterday. To learn balance, I had to make mistakes, learn, adjust and prioritize. This took a level of honesty with myself that was uncomfortable for me. But I was willing to be uncomfortable in order to grow.

Practicing these principles has provided me with the ability to choose. Respond or react? Grow or stay still? Know or ignore God? Without the burden of my own consciousness, and with God as my guide and the principles as my road map, I now have a life brimming with value; a life that has taken an extraordinary evolution. I am respected professionally and in my community. I have strong bonds with family and friends and a partner to share my life with. I have peace and I know serenity, and I have a desire to share it with anyone willing to accept it.

In five short years, I have transformed from that broken girl into a complete, content woman. We truly do live in the age of miracles.

A Message of Hope, a Promise of Freedom

Greg K. (Punanai 2010)

I am writing this letter from Millhaven Federal Penitentiary. I feel blessed that I have been asked to share part of my story with you. My experience is that I am an addict/alcoholic and cannot safely take a drug or drink. My strength comes from my Higher Power, my family, Renascent and 12-step fellowships. My hope can be found written on my medallions — that no addict seeking recovery need die.

I was a 32-year-old man when I acquired 30 charges, which led me to face a possible 15-year prison sentence. This realization brought me to my knees and I finally decided to ask for help. I gave up on the addict's prayer, "God, get me out of this and I swear I'll never do it again." Instead, I said a real prayer: "Help."

My spiritual awakening started right away for me even though I had no idea that was what they were. I was given two choices: treatment or jail. This was a hard decision that I had to think about, because there are drugs and alcohol in jail, and my friends were there. But God was there. He put an angel in front of me who said, "Do you like to kiss and hug me? Well, you can't do that behind bars and visitor's glass in jail."

I made the call to Renascent with the love of my girlfriend, the direction of my parents and the guidance of my "Higher Power." I was told to come to the Punanai Centre the next day and a bed would be ready for me. Something happened in that house that changed my life. People like me shared their stories, and these were "counsellors." I had never heard of a 12-step program before and my view of that was simple: rehab is for quitters.

I couldn't have been more wrong. After 21 days in the house and completing Continuing Care, Renascent armed me with a set of books and sent me back in the wild. The wild for me was house arrest, daily 12-step meetings and staying connected to Renascent through the Alumni Program. I did community-based volunteerism and started to attend church on Sundays with my dad. I also did service work to keep me out of my head, and spent the balance of my time working with my sponsor, which eventually led to full-time employment after some amends were made. I was on top of the world at this point in my journey.

Thirty-one months later, I found myself standing in front of a judge waiting to be sentenced. I thought, as did many others, that with all the changes I had made in myself, there was no way the judge, not to mention God, would send me back to jail. Once again, I was wrong!

As the judge handed me my sentence, I saw the pain and suffering I had caused my family and friends by the stunned looks on their faces. I was also able to see something else: relief that finally they could move on with their lives. With a sentence given, they had a date when they could get their son, friend and family back together. But being an addict, I forgot the tools and fell into the "poor me" syndrome, with a side of the "blame game." Why did God send me to jail? Thank God it would be temporary.

Sitting in my cell on a Thursday afternoon, a lady stopped by and handed me the Basic Text of Narcotics Anonymous and the Big Book of Alcoholics Anonymous. After reading a few pages, I realized what was wrong with me. Since I had been put in jail, I had stopped praying and meditating. I started immediately. Very soon, I was transported to Millhaven and began asking about 12-step meetings. I was informed they were on Thursdays. As Thursday after Thursday passed, and the meetings were cancelled, I became discouraged and began to pray a little harder and a little longer and that's when the miracle happened.

While walking at yard, I was explaining my situation to another inmate when he said to me, "Rehab is for quitters and nobody likes a quitter." Talk about looking at myself in the mirror. It was the new me talking to the old me. What a relief — God had answered my prayers and given me the direction to take. I can often tell God's will today by how I feel in my heart. When I meditate or listen for an answer to a problem, it comes right away and it's usually my will. If the answer comes to me over a period of time and when I'm not thinking about it, that's when it's almost always God's will.

It was at this time that I remembered that it takes only two addicts to have a meeting. So I went on a mission to find the man who had told me about the Thursday 12-step meetings. Armed with my two books, I found him and we had our very own meeting. He soon passed on the info and others started to attend. We now have four or five people every week who meet to find the solution.

I have a message and a promise to pass on. My message is one of hope and my promise is freedom. The hope comes from an acronym: Help Other People Everyday. This hope to me is a big part of Step Twelve; after all, to keep what I have, I must freely give it away. The promise is freedom from active addiction; the solution that escaped my life for so many years. Living within this solution has given me a spiritual awakening that I never thought possible. We do recover; we will be freed from our personal prisons.

I think God sent me to the right place to find others who need recovery. It's my job to find the ones who want it and try to carry the message to the still-suffering addict. My personal experience shows me that it is our actions and what we do with the life we are given that are important. We leave the results with our Higher Power.

I've heard it said, *I am not the man I ought to be, I am not the man I wish to be, and I am not the man I hope to be, but by the grace of God, I am not the man I used to be.*

I am an addict.
Member of River of Freedom.
My name is Greg K.

About Renascent

Over the last 45 years, Renascent has helped more than 45,000 Canadians find hope and healing in recovery from addiction.

The Renascent Fellowship was founded in 1970 by Paul J. Sullivan and a group of businessmen, half of whom were recovering alcoholics, with the goal of opening a new type of treatment centre. Renascent's centre would be a 12-step, abstinence-based and gender-specific drug and alcohol recovery program.

On October 20, 1971, our first client, Donald, walked through the doors of Renascent. Tens of thousands of clients would follow him throughout the following decades.

The Renascent Foundation was incorporated in 1983 to enhance funding for the treatment of alcoholism and drug addiction and ensure that no one would be turned away for lack of funds. With the support of the Foundation, Renascent began to offer programs for families whose loved ones struggle with the illness of addiction.

Today, Renascent owns and operates four centres: the Paul J. Sullivan Centre for men in Brooklin, the Punanai Centre for men in Toronto, the Graham Munro Centre for women in Toronto, and the Lillian and Don Wright Family Health Centre in Toronto — home to our head office and family programs.

Still fiercely committed to 12-step, abstinence-based treatment, Renascent is changing the conversation about addiction and recovery in Canada. Renascent battles the family disease of alcoholism and drug addiction by helping the entire family, including kids. The largest residential treatment centre in Ontario, Renascent's treatment programs are trauma-informed and concurrent-capable; relapse prevention and family care services are available over the phone to ensure distance is never a barrier. Renascent was fully accredited in 2014, meeting standards of excellence assessed by external, non-biased reviewers.

Renascent offers immediate and affordable access to treatment within 24 hours. Donors, working together with our provincial funding partner (Toronto Central LHIN), safeguard public access for the 80% of Canadians who cannot afford treatment. At Renascent, we are passionate about the promise of recovery and we believe that recovery must be available for all who seek it.

24/7 Recovery Helpline: 1-866-232-1212

www.renascent.ca

Renascent
The road to recovery starts here.

Made in the USA
Charleston, SC
28 September 2015